THE MONKEES TALE

By Eric Lefcowitz

LAST GASP

Design by James Stark

ACKNOWLEDGEMENTS

Although duly noted I would like to thank again the photographers who contributed their work to this book: Michael "T" Ventura, Henry Diltz, Jim Marshall, David Gahr, Chester Simpson, Nona Hatay and Susan Holderfield. All album cover reproductions photographed by Linda S. Johnson. Further thanks to Maggie McManus, Gary Strobl, Sandel DeMastus and Jodi Hammrich — all of whom contributed photos and a lot of encouragement. A special thank you to Harold Bronson who conducted all the interviews attributed to Rhino Records. These invaluable interviews were conducted right after the Monkees' break-up by Mr. Bronson. Other help provided by Dave Zimmer, Andrew Rogers and Alan Press. Thank you to Ron Turner, Bob Davis and everyone at Last Gasp. Special thanks to those in the Monkees organization who granted interviews: Michael Dolenz, David Jones, Michael Nesmith, Peter Tork, Bert Schneider, Bob Rafelson, Chip Douglas, Bobby Hart, James Frawley, Lester Sill and others... Bobby Dick and Rodney Bingenheimer (thanks for the ROQing photos). Thanks, Mom and Dad, for not raising a scholar. And a toast to the two people without whom "The Monkees Tale" would never have been completed: Anita Sethi and Duane Dimock. D.T.T.O.I.L. — A.S. Party on, all!

TABLE OF CONTENTS

PREFACE

That the Monkees have earned their niche in the pantheon of popular culture is no longer in doubt. What has remained unwritten, thus far, is a careful dissection of this man-made phenomenon. Words like "plastic" and "exploitative" are often bandied about in the quasi-scholarly analyses that have reached print thus far on the Monkees. "The Monkees Tale," in many ways, is the flip side to these commonly-held notions in that it seeks to set down a journalistic representation of the facts.

In no way, however, can anyone who was not in Don Kirshner's hotel room when Michael Nesmith punched a hole in the wall, claim to have scribed the scripture. The fact that all four Monkees and their two producers agreed to ruminate over their past neatly side-steps any charges, I believe, that "The Monkees Tale" is merely one person's interpretation of what actually happened. This is not to say, on the other hand, that the author's opinions failed to slip into the mix, as you shall read.

What is so often overlooked in books of this kind is that phenomenons like the Monkees — and everything from Elvis to the Archies — represent more than their often-debatable impact on our merry-go-round-and-round pop culture. To the majority of people, the Monkees stand for nothing more than fun. In no insignificant way, they are emblematic of our rose-colored predilection for all things past, which, when all is said and done, is far less destructive than, say, an MX missile.

So, in the best tradition of Messrs. Barnum and Bailey: you paid your two bits — have fun.

Eric Lefcowitz
San Francisco 1985

INTRODUCTION

"Hey, hey we are the Monkees,
To that we all agree,
A manufactured image,
With no philosophies"
        —The "Ditty Diego" Chant from "Head" [1]

The maniacal intent of these wickedly self-mocking words from the Monkees' 1968 movie classic "Head" came far too late to rescue the group's disastrous public image. The Monkees had fought valiantly and honorably to reverse their fortunes, to convince a skeptical public that they really did have something to offer, but the obstacles were too great. To nearsighted pop purists, the chapter had already been closed. The Monkees represented nothing more than a fast-buck cash-in on Beatlemania. No apologies were asked and no quarter was given. The word was out — the Monkees were a disposable pre-fab four, intended only for teenyboppers. And that was that.

In retrospect, it is bewildering how such righteous furor could be generated over such a harmless concept. But like the best of all pop phenomena, the Monkees were both worshipped and vilified. Millions of people, particularly those in the vanguard of the aquarian age, could not — and likely will never — accept the Monkees as a valid, creative enterprise. And yet millions did and still do. Unfortunately, the wet-panty adulation of teenage girls amounted to very little, except money, when stacked up against the media machine's hired guns.

Somehow the informed public missed the innovative wit of the Monkees' TV series, ignored the endearing efforts of their best records and stayed away in droves from the darkly satiric "Head." Instead, they focused directly on the Monkees' manufactured image. Once evidence of their plastic roots was exposed, the Monkees faced a public execution never since witnessed in the colorful annals of popdom. Eventually, the hew and cry came crashing down — like McCarthyism before and Watergate after — into a still-smoldering morass of allegations, counter-allegations, character assassination and lawsuits.

Nearly twenty years later, the smoke screen has finally lifted on the Monkees phenomenon. What remains is a telling portrait of a time when authenticity — a key slogan of the era — could be used as a tool of repression. Instead of simply being accepted at face value, the Monkees were victimized both by their image and an unwritten law stating that all celebrities must scratch and claw their way to fame.

Admittedly, the group was a synthetic creation. Scientifically manufactured in the image of the Beatles, the Monkees were rock's first test-tube baby. And yet the group's illegitimate origins are hardly scandalous considering the roots of rock 'n' roll, which, arguably, is the bastard form of all folk music anyway. This somewhat spurious notion of authenticity clearly muddles the issue. Everyone knows the Monkees cashed in on Beatlemania — the question is, were they artistically bankrupt as well? The answer is on the record.

Not only did the Monkees crank out a bevy of well-regarded pop songs, an Emmy-award winning TV series and a cult-status motion picture, but they left behind a legacy that still affects us today. How often is it reported that Jack Nicholson and Jimi Hendrix both got their first big breaks via the Monkees? Or that the groundbreaking film "Easy Rider" was financed by money made from the Monkees? Outside Hollywood, how many people know that Bob Rafelson and Bert Schneider, the two masterminds behind the Monkees, went on to produce "Five Easy Pieces" and "The Last Picture Show"?

Such questions are moot considering the oft-printed misperception that Don Kirshner was the brains behind the entire enterprise. Even today, few people realize that the four Monkees eventually wrote, produced and performed their own music. Such is the luck of an overnight phenomenon. "There was a willingness on the part of the press to believe that a phenomenon on the scale of the Monkees could be manufactured," explains Michael Nesmith. "But it can't be. Let me tell you, if they could do it, they would. But it's not manufacturable. When it gets up into a certain level it has to have within it its own breathing life."

Part of the confusion, no doubt, stems from the two separate entities called the Monkees or, if you will, Monkees #1 and Monkees #2. Monkees #1 were an incorporated rock 'n' roll band scientifically assembled for network television. As such, they took in millions of dollars for an intricate corporate network that included Screen Gems, RCA Victor, NBC and Kelloggs. Even Kool-Aid had a piece of the action. The Monkees #2 were four entertainers named David Jones,

Micky Dolenz, Peter Tork and Michael Nesmith, who together became a textbook example of overnight superstardom. Although trapped inside the machinery of their attendant fame, the Monkees #2 eventually managed to rise above their mechanical circumstances and take arms against their image.

Taken together, the integrity of the Monkees (both #1 and #2) is irrefutable, especially when one considers the schlock potential of such a venture. And yet the Monkees are still derided in some quarters, nearly two decades later. It is time then to set the record straight: Monkeemania may not have been Beatlemania, but for a brief shining moment in the heady days of 1967, it came precariously close. The Beatles, after all, had only perfected a formula unwittingly discovered by Elvis Presley; that is, incorporating the tried-and-true elements of radio, records, concerts and films with an untested essence: rock 'n' roll. The galvanizing effect of this union was mind-boggling, but, then again, hardly the stuff of genius. At the outset, the hysteria of Beatlemania had generally overshadowed the Beatles' genius. Art or artifice, it mattered little to the screaming throngs of pubescence. Only later, after weathering much ridicule, would the Beatles' genius be detected.

February 9, 1964: A really big shew. Ed and the Fab Four plant the seed.

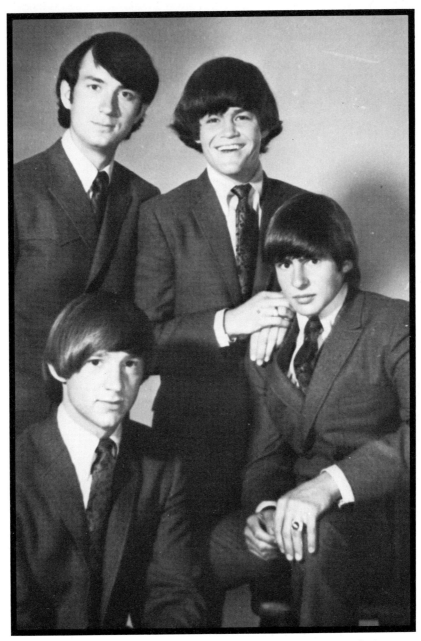

An early publicity shot, circa 1965, of the Monkees. First and foremost, they were a video group. (From the collection of Maggie McManus)

And so it was with the Monkees, except they added one more feature to the formula: television. Oddly enough, save for the Ed Sullivan Show's legendary appearances of Elvis and the Beatles (interesting how square-looking guys like Ed can alter the history of rock 'n' roll), the immense power of television as a promotional tool had lain dormant since its inception. The opportunistic tandem of Rafelson and Schneider adroitly foresaw the kinetic possibilities of an untapped goldmine. But true to the times (1965-68), these particular producers had no desire to market a crass, insubstantial product — the kids wouldn't buy it. So they designed a show that snapped, crackled and popped with the latest new-wave techniques and talent.

"There was a natural bent for rebellion that was in the air at the time that created a new effort in television. Things didn't have to be so plotted," Rafelson recalls. "People who were eight or nine years old look back on the show and remember there was something different about it — it bombarded their senses." Underneath the helter-skelter histrionics, however, lurked a subtle anarchism that jelled with the Monkees' youthful viewing audience.

"It wasn't 'Father Knows Best,'" Schneider contends, "it was the kids know best. The heroes were young people and the heavies were older people." By appealing to the previously verboten inner reaches of teenage fantasy life, "The Monkees" show managed to stray outside the stale mid-American mores that sitcoms represented.

As the pre-teens nurtured on Monkeemania gradually grow older, their appreciation of the basically good-natured Monkees phenomenon seems to grow proportionately. "The reason that the Monkees meant so much to so many people, I think, was because, without threatening them, there seemed to be an element of this is the way things could be," reasons Tork. "It was part of the Sixties' all you need is love notion and some people are going to be stuck in the Sixties for the rest of their lives."

Beyond the warm glow of nostalgia, however, is a prophetic role that Monkees played in the current rock video revolution on television. On every episode, the Monkees performed two new songs in free-form visual romps that closely resemble the video clip techniques now hailed as state-of-the-art. Years before the advent of MTV and formats of similar ilk, the Monkees proved the dynamic potential of the visual image. The proof was in the pudding: when the show was running, Monkees discs sold faster than acne products; once the show was cancelled, sales took a nose dive.

"It was the demonstration of these two giant media complexes pooling their resources and promoting something together," Dolenz explains. "It wouldn't have mattered if it was the Monkees or a particular brand of soap. It was the first time in the history of the industries that the two got in bed together and pushed a common project."

Jones remembers, "the critics were arguing which came first the chicken or the egg — the music or the TV? Well, obviously the fact that we didn't have to go onto American Bandstand to promote our new single answers the question. We just sang it on our TV show each week."

In the future, as the video revolution gradually transforms the music industry into a visual medium, the Monkees' legacy will continue to grow in stature. Only recently has credit long overdue been accorded to the Monkees. "It was something that was little understood then, maybe better understood now, but I don't think it will be completely understood until many years later," Nesmith remarks about the video contributions of the Monkees. "There was a type of power, a seed that was planted, that was beyond the obvious manufactured image, that was beyond 'let's exploit the Beatles phenomenon.' And it had to do with contemporary music and film at the time — there was a collective psychological shift in the thinking of television and how it approached music. It was a marriage that came together in a unique and certain wonderful way and, in the future, people will look back and realize that."

Despite some inspired musical moments, the Monkees were first and last a video group. For those who scoff at Beatles comparisons, consider for a moment the argument in terms of visual, rather than musical, output. In this scenario, the underrated Monkees episodes, taken as a whole, certainly match the innovation and ingenuity of the Beatles' first two films, "A Hard Day's Night" and "Help!" The psychedelic underpinnings of the Monkees' TV special, "33 1/3 Revolutions Per Monkee," ring far truer than the bathetic "Magical Mystery Tour." And the cinema verité viewpoint in "Let It Be" is positively moribund when compared to the cutting sardonicism of the Monkees' only motion picture, "Head."

Altogether, of course, the Beatles were far more culturally significant than the Monkees. No argument there. Nonetheless, the two groups share the distinction of having risen above the mania they spawned. This book is the tale of the Monkees and the trappings of their meteoric rise to fame, but it begins, appropriately, with the Beatles. . . .

EVOLUTION

~~~~~~

When John Lennon uttered the immortal words "we're more popular than Jesus," the bible-thumpers of America vented their wrath through ritualized Beatle burnings. In truth, Lennon had only said what many already knew — rock 'n' roll had become the divine belief of a disembodied generation. The Beatles were the shining stars of this new and unexplored galaxy of youth culture. They had risen almost magically from the decay of Liverpool to a tumult rivalled only by Elvis. In retrospect, Beatlemania seems a natural and thoroughly inevitable result of the times: JFK's presidency and assassination, the decline of Elvis as a rebel hero, the rise of suburbia, and a baby-boom market ripe for consumption.

By August 29, 1966, the thrill was gone — the Beatles had grown tired of Beatlemania. That night, they performed their very last live gig at Candlestick Park in San Francisco. Now at the height of their popularity, the fabulous foursome needed something else (that apparently being LSD) to fuel their creative drive. Within months they would announce this change with a single that would revolutionize rock music — "Penny Lane"/"Strawberry Fields."

While striving beyond the parameters of pop, the Beatles had left something in their wake: a mania gap. Sure, there were other fab groups — the Stones, the DC5, Herman's Hermits, the Kinks — who had the image, but none had the collective identity of John, Paul, George and Ringo.

Two weeks before the Beatles' last show, a new American group named the Monkees had emerged with "Last Train To Clarksville." A snappy, expertly produced single, "Clarksville" was an instant hit. Only industry insiders knew who or what the Monkees were at this time. To the public, the group probably seemed anything but unique; after all, they already had the Crickets, the Byrds, the Animals and the Chipmunks (who could forget Simon, Alvin and Theodore?). Another addition to this menagerie was hardly cause for celebration.

In America, despite a plethora of homegrown rock bands, no Yankee counterparts had toppled the British Invasion. The Beach Boys, the Beau Brummels and Paul Revere and the Raiders had made some inroads, but none had achieved the proper balance of mystique and musicianship that was necessary to create a phenomenon.

The masterminds of Raybert, Bob Rafelson (left) and Bert Schneider, plotting the phenomenon. (Photo by Henry Diltz)

That's precisely what Bob Rafelson and Bert Schneider had set out to do: create a phenomenon. The two producers, both in their mid-thirties, had originally met in New York in the late 1950's. Rafelson was a freelance director who had worked for, among others, ABC and Desilu; Schneider was biding time as a Screen Gems liaison. Together, they fostered a friendship and, after relocating to Los Angeles in the early 1960's, a lucrative business partnership as well.

Out of 437 applicants, the four finalists. At this point, they were happy just to have a steady job.
(From the collection of Jodi Hammrich)

The maverick duo struck a keen equilibrium — both possessed a nonconformist bent in business that would mark their work for a decade to come. The political savvy of Schneider balanced perfectly with Rafelson's sense of the insouciant. Schneider had built a reputation as a compellingly honest upper-management tactician who knew how to straddle both sides of an issue for the common good. Rafelson had an uncanny knack for spotting unrefined talent. Both men were creative dynamos with an ineffable love of the outrageous.

Together, under the appellation of Raybert Productions, the pair set up headquarters in Hollywood. Their initial aim as Raybert was to gather enough capital to bankroll motion picture productions. Then and now, quick money could be had in the cathode-ray tube known as television. "Our ambitions were to make movies," Schneider explains. "We began with a TV series because that was the foot in the door. It was easier to get a pilot of a TV series made than it was to get a movie made." Thus, the duo turned to rock 'n' roll. Their first project was the Monkees.

How and why Schneider picked the moniker "The Monkees" is hardly worth a deep, psychoanalytic probe. It was not, however, his only choice. "We kind of fooled around with 'The Creeps,' " Schneider told the *Saturday Evening Post*, "but we decided it was too negative." Other names, such as the Turtles and the Inevitables, were briefly bandied about before a final decision. Why Monkees? "I don't know why," Schneider quipped to the *Post*, "I'll have to ask my analyst."

Despite the Monkees' apparent and oft-attributed lineage to the Beatles, Rafelson, to this day, contends his inspiration predated the Beatles' debut on the silver screen. "I had the idea for the Monkees years before the Beatles arrived," insists Rafelson. "I tried to sell it as a folk-rock group, something about which I knew because I had travelled with a group of unruly and somewhat chaotic musicians in Mexico in 1953. We were itinerant musicians and I used many of the incidents that happened to me in Mexico in the Monkees episodes.

"So that's where the idea began. I wrote it as a pilot for Universal in the early Sixties before rock 'n' roll had entrenched. But I had a hard time selling it until the Beatles came along and lent credence to the popularity, not only of the music, but of using film in the fashion it was being used them. After all, [Richard] Lester was a director of commercials at the time and was really borrowing heavily from nouvelle French techniques."

Unlike Rafelson, Schneider readily acknowledges the Beatles' influence on the genesis of the Monkees. "The Beatles made it all happen, that's the reality," Schneider says. "Richard Lester is where the credit begins for the Monkees and for Bob and me."

Whatever the origins of the species, the Monkees were an idea that could hardly miss. "American Bandstand" and "Hullaballoo" had long since proved the economic viability of rock'n'roll on television. So when former child star Jackie Cooper, then an official of Screen Gems, allocated $225,000 to Raybert for a Monkees pilot film in late '65, he hardly qualified as visionary. Screen Gems, in fact, was the television branch of Columbia Pictures, the entertainment conglomerate headed by Abe Schneider, father of Bert.

The problem now was caging the proper primates. At first, Rafelson and Schneider scoured Hollywood for an existing rock act that would fit the bill. Among those auditioned were the Lovin' Spoonful. Nothing clicked, however, prompting the duo to seek out their desired Monkees via a trade paper advertisement. On September 8, 1965, the now-historic ad appeared in *Daily Variety*:

Madness!!
Auditions
Folk & Rock Musicians-Singers
For Acting Roles in New TV Series
Running Parts for 4 Insane Boys, Age 17-21
Want Spirited Ben Frank's Types
Have Courage To Work
Must Come Down For Interview

Hidden within the ad were several in-jokes designed to weed out the chaff. "Ben Franks" was a reference to a popular Sunset Strip eatery where the mods mused over burgers and fries. "Must come down," according to Rafelson, was "a sly reference to being high."

In all probability, these cryptic allusions mattered little to the 437 work-starved applicants that swamped Raybert's office. Everybody who was anybody in L.A. took a crack at the auditions, including the cream of burgeoning rock scene. Among those who tried out were Harry Nilsson and Paul Williams (both of whom later penned songs for the Monkees), Danny Hutton (later of Three Dog Night), and 434 others. According to L.A.'s legendary DJ, Rodney Bingenheimer, none other than Charles Manson took a stab at the job. Unfortunately, Manson could not be reached for comment.

Perhaps the most notorious of the Monkees might-have-beens was Stephen Stills, who got as far as a screen test before failing. As legend would have it, Stills lost out due to a receding hairline and a recessed tooth. In Dave Zimmer's biography of Crosby, Stills and Nash, however, Stills argues to the contrary. "They could have fixed my teeth," claims Stills. "What I really wanted to do was write songs for the show. But I found out that I'd have to give up my publishing and that they already had a pair of staff writers in Boyce and Hart."

Schneider remembers that Stills "had a little less abandon. In order to do this kind of thing, guys really had to have a lot of abandon. I suspect Stephen was a little bit more inhibited."

Ironically, it was Stills who recommended Peter Tork for the role he eventually landed. "Stephen was the guy who looked like me on Greenwich Village streets," Tork told Goldmine magazine. "That's how I recognized him: I walked up to him and said, 'You're the guy that looks like me.' And he said, 'Oh, you're the guy I'm supposed to look like.' So, when they were looking for somebody like him but whose hair and teeth were better, Stephen instantly thought of his friend Peter, threw the bone his way, and took for a consolation prize the Buffalo Springfield and Crosby, Stills, Nash and Young. Poor guy."

Contrary to popular belief, only one of the final four Monkees actually saw the infamous ad — Michael Nesmith. David Jones was already under contract at Columbia, Micky Dolenz found out through his agent and Tork heard from Stills.

At the auditions, all four managed to wend their way through and intricate and pressure-filled process of elimination. Rafelson, who wrote his college thesis on cultural anthropology, utilized his skills in waging a psychological war among applicants. Only the fittest would survive. After filling out a questionnaire, the 437 hopefuls were lead unknowingly to the offices of Rafelson and Schneider. Once there, the applicants faced a series of intimidation tactics designed to expose their real identities. According to an article that later appeared in the *Saturday Evening Post*, "many applicants becme flustered when caught in the crossfire as the producers staged mock arguments over their merits, or ignored them while playing catch with a golf ball."

Two actors (Dolenz and Jones) meet two musicians (Tork and Nesmith). The question was, would they harmonize?

In a recent interview, Rafelson defended his confrontational tactics, remarking that, "as a rule, actors come into an audition prepared. Usually they've heard very little about the project that's real. For example, their agents, who don't know anything, have told them they're looking for somebody sexy. So the girl comes into your office and tries to be sexy. The thing is to unmask those people as quickly as possible to find out who they are. This is what we did with the Monkees."

The final four Monkees each impressed the producers in separate fashion. Nesmith drew a diagonal line through the section of his application inquiring about his previous experience and wrote the word "Life." According to the Post, "Micky Dolenz found Rafelson and Schneider seated on opposite sides of a desk, absorbed in balancing a pile of soda bottles, glasses and paper cups. Impulsively, he snatched a cup off the desk, balanced it on top of the stack and shouted 'Checkmate!' He scored an immediate hit."

Ultimately, the entire process boiled down to screen tests — Hollywood's test of fire. Once again, the applicants faced a volley of unpredictable questions. Two of these screen tests were later grafted onto the pilot episode, which aired in the first season. Both tests are fascinating artifacts that reveal as much about the two subjects, Nesmith and Jones, as they do the off-camera inquisitor, Rafelson.

After taping two dozen screen tests, Rafelson and Schneider mixed and matched the applicants in an effort to band together four members with a balanced separation of style, look and personality. Once they narrowed their choices down to eight finalists, the producers took the screen tests to Audience Studies Incorporated (ASI), a research subsidiary of Screen Gems that measured random samples of a viewing audience and computerized their findings. The final results were tallied: David Jones, Micky Dolenz, Peter Tork and Michael Nesmith were now the Monkees.

Over the years, much ballyhoo has been made over the laboratory Darwinism employed by Rafelson and Schneider. In the end, however, their choices more than justified their means. First and foremost, all four Monkees vindicated Raybert's confidence by evolving into legitimate talents. Furthermore, the bold stroke of casting two actors — Dolenz and Jones — with two musicians — Nesmith and Tork — ultimately elevated the project to greater creative heights as the musicians learned to act and vice-versa. Raybert's decision to cast authentic personalities, rather than professional actors who would imitate teenagers, was yet another masterstroke. Although advised to the contrary, Raybert stuck to their guns. "I would rather work with amateur actors," Rafelson told the New York Times. "If you hired professionals you wouldn't get the primitiveness we were looking for."

Another testament to Raybert's wisdom surfaced later as the four Monkees began to match the temperaments and the appeal of the four Beatles. Jones had the cuddly cuteness of McCartney, Nesmith had the mercurial arrogance of Lennon, Dolenz mirrored the happy-go-lucky Ringo and Tork was similar to the inward, mystical Harrison. Such comparisons meant little to the four Monkees, who were happy at this point to have a steady paycheck. Prior to casting, Tork had been washing dishes for $50 a week, Dolenz had been studying architecture and singing with the Missing Links, Nesmith was a fledgling folk musician with a wife, a child and a broken down station wagon and Jones was a proto-star looking for his lucky break. Thus, the theory that the Monkees never paid their dues was, like so many Monkees legends, nothing more than sour grapes, jealous musicians and uninformed writers.

Only one stone was left unturned by Raybert's arduous casting techniques: would the boys get along? Judging from the nature of the beast, one might anticipate a personality clash from the four headstrong survivors. Although this inevitable tug-of-egos never did materialize, it is probably safe to say that the intrapersonal relations between the four Monkees were tepid at best. "There was always some tension, always some jealousy," Tork confided in a recent interview. "In every group of four there are six pairs — there were six fights, one each."

Due to the pre-scheduling of the pilot, the boys hardly had an opportunity to introduce themselves before commencing shooting in November, 1965. Prior to their casting, Jones and Dolenz had met each other in a studio commissary where both were guest starring on network series (Dolenz on "Route 66," Jones on "Ben Casey"). Nesmith and Tork, too, had briefly crossed paths in an L.A. club. Still, the synergy of the unit remained untested.

In an almost apocryphal incident, the foursome's first social outing nearly careened out of control. After being introduced, the group set out to Dennys to grab some food before filming a Kelloggs commercial. Once there, the conversation split into natural pairs — Nesmith and Tork talked about music, Dolenz and Jones discussed acting. Everyone ordered salads, which all arrived promptly, except Jones'. The other three stabbed ungraciously at their lunches, oblivious to Jones, who watched silently in disgust. After a few minutes, much to everyone's surprise, Jones blurted out, "You guys are pigs — absolute pigs! You can't even eat!" There was an ominous pause as the others, stunned, sat and watched Jones demonstrate what he considered proper etiquette in eating his newly-arrived salad. As he cut the contents up into small, neat pieces, he exclaimed, "Now, this is how one eats a salad" and then picked up the entire portion with his hands and shoveled as much into his mouth as was possible. All four then fell about laughing — the ice had been broken.

If nothing else, this incident illustrates how young the newly-annointed Monkees actually were at this point. Jones was the youngest at nineteen, followed by Dolenz, twenty, Nesmith, twenty-two, and Tork, twenty-three.

Aside from the incalculable risk of putting four assertive young men together, the last-second casting also necessitated a decision that would haunt the project until its dying days — the Monkees would not make their own music. Instead, outside songwriters, specifically Tommy Boyce and Bobby Hart, were commissioned to score the pilot. The repercussions of this move would be felt in the years to come, but, for now, all musical decisions were in the hands of Boyce and Hart. Fresh from the talented stables of New York's latter-day Tin Pan Alley, the Brill Building, Boyce and Hart were a thoroughbred writing team with a knack for knocking out three-minute melodies. Raybert was sufficiently impressed with their talents to hire them for the pilot for which they composed three songs, "The Monkees Theme," "I Wanna Be Free" and "Let's Dance On."

"We had to have those tracks made before the group ever existed," Schneider explains. "I can remember meeting with Boyce and Hart at the same time we were interviewing kids to be in the Monkees. In fact, Boyce and Hart were hoping to be in the group themselves."

As a consequence, in the original pilot the Monkees merely lip-synched to the music and vocals of Boyce and Hart. Later, when the episode finally aired, the voices of the Monkees were dubbed back in. Surprisingly, despite the bitter haggling over musical control that would eventuate, the Monkees uttered not a single word of protest. This is partially due, no doubt, to the sudden whirlwind pace of events in their lives. In less than a week's time, all four had landed their prized roles and had begun filming the pilot episode. In all likelihood, music was the last thing on their minds. Besides, as Schneider maintains, "it was inconceivable that they would have become a cohesive group that fast."

An interesting sidenote that seems to contradict Schneider's assertion was later revealed by Tork in Bruce Pollock's *When The Music Mattered:* "When the Monkees made their pilot, the four of us got on stage and we were supposed to be doing a dance set. Mike had his guitar, I had my bass, Micky knew two beats on the drums. During breaks in filming we asked the stage crew to fire up the amps, and, never having played together before on the same stage, we knocked out a song and the audience liked us. Everyone danced. When it was over they applauded. Some people from Capitol records, who heard us, said they would have signed us even if we hadn't had a TV show."

The pilot not only set the standard in terms of musical direction, but it established the thematic axis as well. The storyline, written by Paul Mazursky (who makes a brief cameo appearance) and Larry Tucker, was fairly simplistic: the Monkees are hired to perform at a sweet-sixteen party. Things go awry when Davy falls in love with the hostess, setting off all sorts of madcap Monkee business. Beyond the skeletal plot, however, lurked a benevolent yet pointedly modern bent to the show. Amidst all the Hollywood hokum of the plotline was a certain incandescent charm and forthrightness unseen elsewhere. The Monkees themselves were portrayed as regular bumbling Joes rather than untouchable rock icons — a thematic ploy which softened the edge of the show's subtle anti-establishment stance.

The visual presentation of "The Monkees" show was also an unexplored entity on network television at the time. Despite their debt to Richard Lester's "A Hard Day's Night" and such silent-screen masters as Charlie Chaplin, Buster Keaton and Mack Sennett, Rafelson and his cohorts brought what was an entirely new language to network programming. Gone was the static visual stylization of sitcoms past. Match cuts and continuity were thrown to the winds. By shooting film, a galaxy of effects were possible. Abrupt cutaways and sped-up action were now de rigueur, adding an almost Dada-esque element to the proceedings. In one freeze-frame sequence at the end of the pilot, a cartoon-like bubble appears next to a dancing nymphet, asking, "a typical teenager?" — only to be answered by another bubble — "no a friend of the producers."

"We came up with every technique we could think of in order to make it visually interesting," remembers James Frawley, director of 28 of the 58 episodes. "We used mirror shots, trick shots, upside-down angles, weird lenses, anything we wanted."

Flat lighting — a typical TV technique whereby the entire set is lit the same — was scrapped altogether. Rafelson explains, "I believed very strongly at the time that background in television counted for nought. All you ever looked at was the foreground because there's no depth to the medium. So I said, 'light the foreground, fuck the background, let's shoot fast and we'll make it in the editing room.' It caused a monumental amount of editing."

Instead of the established twenty-five or so set-ups a day, the Monkees often used as many as ninety. Rafelson's boast to *TV Guide* — I do not regard film as a sacred parchment but as a pliable thing" — became prophesy, particularly in the two musical sequences per episode, which were generally free-form romps. It is Nesmith's contention that the power of these mini-musicals are what contributed to the misperception that "The Monkees" show was pure improvisation. "The magic to the show wasn't the scripts," Nesmith says. "The magic was the muscial numbers and they were almost entirely ad-libbed. But they weren't ad-libbed by us necessarily, they were ad-libbed by Jim Frawley and the camera crew."

"I had the freedom that most directors pray for," Frawley corroborates. "It gave me the kind of autonomy that spoiled me for working with other people because I had absolute and total freedom, which is very nurturing to a young director. If I wanted to shoot an entire episode with one lens just to see what it looked like, I could do that. If I wanted to try cutting experiments, I could do that, too, because every show had a couple of musical numbers which were pretty free-form."

Incorporating six or seven minutes of each episode, the Monkees' musical sequences were revolutionary for their time. Many of the vaunted techniques on modern-day video-clips were first used in the Monkees' romps almost twenty years before the advent of MTV. Paul Mazursky told

(From the collection of Maggie McManus)

The Beatles and the Monkees — two breeds apart. Jones: "If we can only be one quarter as good... or maybe a tenth?"

"Entertainment Tonight" that "The Monkees" show was the "forerunner of the whole notion of the kind of MTV thing that's happening, the fast-gag, the quick move, the wipe, the dissolve, all the old silent film techniques."

At the time, however, doubts still lingered as to whether the public would buy such blasphemy. The first indicators were not promising. In early 1966, Rafelson and Schneider screened the pilot for an ASI test audience. It laid an egg, scoring one of the lowest ratings ever. "What we found in the original testing," Schneider explains, "was for those in the audience who didn't know who these guys were, the anti-establishment stance was too much of an affront to their sensibilities and attitudes. Those kind of testing services bring in the whole demographic, a typical TV audience, so you're going to have all the older people in there as well as the younger. Well, the older peole just hated the kids — you couldn't get past that. In other words, they weren't prepared to see the humor because they had already turned off their minds."

Instead of throwing in the towel, Rafelson immediately took the pilot back into the editing room, where he recut the episode by strategically placing Nesmith and Jones' screen tests at the outset of the show. "I spent 48 straight hours in the editing room" Rafelson recalls, "and put the interviews at the very beginning so people could get to know the Monkees and therefore buy some of their so-called anti-establishment." Rafelson's gamble hit pay-dirt — only two days after the show had bombed, it scored a high enough rating to convince NBC to give it a shot.

The next step was to get the four Monkees, particularly newcomers Nesmith and Tork, ready to face the camera. Under the auspices of Frawley, the group started a six-week improvisational workshop in Screen Gems stage three, where a sign was erected reading "Monkees — Keep Out!" Frawley, who had, up to this time, only directed two experimental films, was skilled in the art of improvisation. As a member of an innovative New York comedy troupe named The Premise, Frawley had honed his talents with the able likes of Buck Henry and George Segal. Still, Frawley was something of a rookie when it came to the Hollywood big leagues.

Publicity still from the pilot episode of the Monkees prophetically lip-synching, "I Wanna Be Free". Notice Jones playing guitar. (From the collection of Jodi Hammrich)

Raybert's confidence in untested talent was indicative of the hell-bent, go-for-broke attitude of the organization. "If you're going in a direction that requires that you be innovative," Schneider explains, "it's impossible to reach into the same pool of talent where everybody else reaches because then you're not going to get innovators, you'll get imitators. Our attitude was 'we're jumping off the bridge here, there's no point in going halfway.' "

As it turns out, Frawley's relative inexperience was perfectly suited to the Monkees, who were more than a little green themselves, and anxious to boot. To loosen them up, Frawley had the boys run through a series of improvisational exercises that found them imitating animals or impersonating celebrities. "These sessions gave the guys a chance to improvise together and to establish a feel of ensemble," says Frawley. "Also, it gave Bob, Bert and me a chance to determine where the strengths and weaknesses of each of the boys lay."

Although rehearsals helped to establish a personal rapport between the four Monkees, the spontaneous anarchy generated in these sessions ultimately resulted in a disastrous incident — one that would permanently damage the show's ratings. In June, 1966, NBC affiliates gathered at Chasens restaurant in Los Angeles to preview the fall line-up. Stars of the new network shows came to parade their wares for local affiliates from across the country. Schneider, figuring that some affiliates from conservative locales might not appreciate the Monkees' brand of humor, had suggested that the boys pass up their appearance. Somehow, for unknown reasons, this advice was ignored as the now-confident Monkees went ahead to the meeting. Once there, the four boys, who were probably under one exotic influence or another, proceeded to make a shambles of the entire affair.

TV Guide later reported the monkeeshines in full detail: "Somebody had dragged along a stuffed peacock. They played volleyball with it, stopping traffic on Beverly Boulevard. Micky got into the restaurant's switch box and turned off all the lights. Finally they were introduced by Dick Clark. Since they hadn't any musical instruments. . . they did 'comedy' material. Micky shaved with the microphone. Davy pretended he was a duck. The jokes began to die."

The network and the show paid dearly for this display. Several affiliates were sufficiently offended by the Monkees' lack of decorum that they rejected the show without seeing it. According to *TV Guide*, at least five key stations failed to pick up the series, which, in turn, resulted in lower national ratings throughout the entire run of the series. As a result, "The Monkees" show, despite its popularity and its Emmys, never cracked the Top 25 in the Nielsen ratings.

Raybert had even bigger problems to deal with, however, as the deadline of their network debut rapidly approached. Where were they going to find enough music to fill up the scheduled thirty-two episodes? Even the prolific team of Boyce and Hart could hardly generate that much music in so short a time. There was only one human who could tackle such a dilemma — the Man With The Golden Ear: Don Kirshner.

Kirshner, as the Monkees would soon discover, was truly a double-edged sword. There was no denying the man's almost supernatural knack for divining the latest boffo smash hits, but Kirshner was hardly reticent when it came to taking credit, either. His boast to *Time* — "I can hear a kid hit a note and I know whether he has it or not" — best illustrates the problematic nature of Kirshner's personality. On the one hand, there was Kirshner the infallible hitmaker. On the other hand, there was Kirshner the megalomaniac. "Kirshner had an ego that transcended everything else," Schneider contends. "It's sad because it was that ego of his that caused real conflicts and ended up in a very bad fight with the group."

Kirshner's conceit was not entirely unfounded. At 32, he was the hottest music publisher in the business, having sold over 150 million recordings. As president of the music division of Columbia Pictures/Screen Gems TV, he lorded over a virtual goldmine of songwriting talent, including Carole King, Neil Sedaka, Gerry Goffin, Barry Mann, Cynthia Weil and Neil Diamond.

Donnie — as all the hipsters in the biz called him — had nurtured the Brill Building pop sound with extraordinary managerial aplomb. Amazingly, he did this with nary a musical bone in his body. "Kirshner plays only one instrument," *Time* reported, "the telephone. There are 14 of them in his South Orange, N.J., home, and an eleven-channel radiophone in his chauffeured Fleetwood."

As a teenager growing up in the Bronx, Kirshner and his pal Robert Walden Cassotto (later Bobby Darin) had taken a crack at writing commercial jingles. They failed. In 1958, however, Kirshner formed The Aldon Music publishing company with partner Al Nevins, capitalizing on the songwriting talents of Neil Sedaka and Howie Greenfield. After amassing a small fortune, Kirshner sold the company in 1963 to Columbia Pictures, where he now functioned as musical supervisor over such TV shows as "Bewitched" and "I Dream Of Jeannie." By the time Schneider called in the summer of 1966 and pleaded, "Donnie, we need a miracle!" Kirshner's Midas touch had tarnished in comparison to his previous peaks. He instantly recognized the Monkees as a perfect vehicle for regaining his stature within the industry. "When I did the Monkees," Kirshner explained in *The Making Of Superstars*, "the Beatles were getting married. They weren't touchable to the public anymore; they lost their innocence. I knew that if a group like the Monkees came on TV, it would take all the marbles."

Within 18 hours, Kirshner had performed the miracle that Schneider requested — he flew out to L.A. with twelve demo records that were ready to roll. Under Kirshner's guidance, the Monkees need only dub their voices over pre-recorded tracks which were cranked out with Henry Ford efficiency. Still, even this relatively uncomplicated procedure turned out to be a prickly task. "We were all real nervous about it," Kirshner told *The Making Of Superstars*. "They were pre-stars and were a little frightened about being on TV. I was there to do business because I had records to get out. So I walked in with four ringers — four studio men —because I assumed the Monkees would give me a hard time. And after they clowned around for the first ten minutes, I said, 'All right, fellas — out!' And I brought in the four ringers. I put them on the mikes and the boys came back right away and we made some great records together."

From the very start, the Monkees had made the recording process anything but smooth. In the realm of television they were, except for Dolenz, relative neophytes and therefore acquiescent. In the studio, however, the artistic temperaments of Nesmith and Tork strained matters considerably. Part of the tension resulted from the musical positions each member would assume. Nobody wanted to be hidden behind the drums, least of all Nesmith, who insisted on guitar. Jones, of course, was far too small. Finally, Dolenz reluctantly agreed to take up the skins, in spite of their theatrical liability.

Already the boys had disposed of such producers as Snuffy Garrett, Mickie Most and Carole King, who reportedly left the studio in tears. By process of elimination, Boyce and Hart inherited the unenviable task of producing the group. Hart remembers, "all this time we were tugging at Donnie's sleeves. Finally after all of these fiascos, time was short, the show was going on the air and they needed to have a record out, so we [Boyce and Hart] got the job. As a result, Hart's band, the Candy Store Prophets, were brought in as session players and the ball got rolling.

Contrary to popular belief, the Monkees did have a chance to go into the recording studio alone, although Tork later told the *Saturday Evening Post*, "we were directionless and unproductive, musically speaking." Considering their brief tenure as an ensemble and the disparate musical styles each member brought into the project, these results were practically inevitable. Rafelson explains, "groups as rule, up until this time, took years of consolidation on the streets. A bass player meets a drummer — they join one group, they pick up another guitarist, they move over to another group, they fire two guys until finally it gets consolidated, just like the Beatles, over a long period of time. A harmonious sense of what the sound should be is born of a lot of trial and error. Well, these guys never had that opportunity and so for them to find out what kind of music they wanted to create and who was going to be the boss was a bit of a jumble."

The tapes of the Monkees' maiden efforts in the studio were sent to Kirshner, who later told *TV Guide*, "I heard them. They were loud... It was not the right sound of today. I wanted a musical sex image. Something you'd recognize next time you heard it. Davy was OK — for musical comedy. Mike was the weakest singer as far as I was concerned. Micky was a natural mimic. And he had the best voice for our purposes."

Only a few days after being hired, Kirshner had made his mark on the Monkees. Now there were 22 songs — enough for the first five episodes and a debut album — where, prior to hiring Kirshner, there had been only three. Furthermore, as head of Columbia/Screen Gems' music division, Kirshner negotiated a partnership with RCA Victor, who would distribute Monkees records under a newly-formed label named Colgems.

"The Monkees" show was swiftly becoming the Don Kirshner show, an image that Kirshner did little to prevent. Kirshner was particularly autocratic in the studio, where he prized over his vinyl Frankenstein. His method was best described in the *Saturday Evening Post*: "In the control room, Kirshner presided over a maze of dials, switches and levers rising from a bulky, two-ton console worthy of Dr. Strangelove. The push of a red button activated an echo chamber which embellished the singers' faint voices. By pulling a switch, hunks of harmony were automatically superimposed over previously recorded Monkees solos. 'Whatever is irritating or jarring,' says Kirshner, 'you can just bury electronically.'"

Boyce and Hart's "Last Train To Clarksville," the first Colgems release, is a sterling example of Kirshner's talents. The song itself is a catchy, if unremarkable, three-chord ditty, but under Kirshner's direction it becomes a patchwork of deft edits and electronic trickery. Certain moments, including the jangling guitar break and several stop-on-a-dime pauses, transform the song from mundane to electrifying. Although it is difficult to speculate on such matters, "Clarksville" may well have been a hit without any television exposure.

RCA Victor, however, was taking no chances. The record company forked out the then-formidable sum of $100,000 to promote the band. A team of 76 advance men were commissioned to saturate the market with media hype. Bumper stickers proclaiming "Monkee Business Is Big Business" were distributed across the county. Flyers were handed out at Beatles' concerts. Preview records were sent to six thousand disc jockeys.

All in all, the advance hype had reached a fever pitch. Everybody wanted a piece of the action, despite the fact that the show had yet to air. Tommy Boyce remembers the anticipatory excitement: "All the corporate people flew in from around the world to Hollywood and said, 'what's the first record going to be? Whatever it is, it will be number one in three weeks.'"

On August 16, 1966, "Last Train To Clarksville"/"Take A Giant Step" was released on the

Don Kirshner (center) lends a golden ear to the future Monkee tunesmiths Tommy Boyce (left) and Bobby Hart. Notice wall photo of Kirshner meeting JFK. (Photo by David Gahr)

virginal Colgems label. The top album on the charts was the Beatles' "Yesterday and Today" and the number one song was the Lovin Spoonful's "Summer In The City." But if any doubts lingered regarding the competition, they were quelled in *Billboard's* review of "Clarksville": "All the excitement generated by the promotional campaign... is justified by this debut disk loaded with exciting teen dance beats."

The thoroughness of the publicity campaign was further evidenced when the Monkees made their first public appearance on September 9th at the Broadway Theatre in New York. In front of an audience described by Vince Canby of the *New York Times* as "too old for Barbie dolls and too young for mini-skirts," the Monkees merely took the stage and introduced themselves. Rafelson remembers the reaction: "There was so much hoopla about the coming show, with ads on TV, and kids were so quick to attach themselves to fads, that when the Monkees came to New York, absent their instruments, it was pandemonium. All they did was stand there and introduce themselves."

Rafelson and Schneider had been vindicated — success was all but guaranteed. In four days, the show would debut on nationwide television and already "Clarksville" had sold 400,000 copies. It had been exactly one year and one day since they had advertised for "four insane boys" and wound up with 437. Had they picked the right ones? Would the networks buy it? More importantly, would the kids buy it? By now the answers were obvious.

"You can fool some of the kids some of the time," Rafelson chortled to the *Times*. Little did he know, the best was yet to come.

Each Monkee got a customized Pontiac GTO with four bucket seats. Nesmith, symbolically, is at the wheel.

THE FIRST SEASON

At 7:30 PM EST on Monday, September 12, 1966, "The Monkees" show debuted in living color on NBC. With the trill of a tomtom, the finger-popping beat of "The Monkees Theme" announced their arrival with ominous forebodence:

"Anytime or anywhere,
Just look over your shoulder,
Guess who'll be standing there,
Hey, hey we're the Monkees!" 2

Initial rating surveys were less encouraging than expected, a fact partially attributed to the damage wrought at the network previews. Another factor in the disappointing returns was the series' head-to-head competition with ABC's "Gilligan's Island," a sacred cow among teenagers. For discerning cognoscenti, the grave decision whether to watch "The Monkees" or "Gilligan's Island" was akin to choosing between Bach and Handel. All this, fair reader, in the prehistoric times B.V. (Before VCRs).

In contrast to the ratings, the show's reviews were glowing. The *Los Angeles Times* raved about moments of ingenuity, while the *New York Times* claimed the Monkees were "the Marx Brothers in adolescence," noting that "progress can turn up in the strangest places."

Other reviewers tempered their enthusiasm, however, with back-handed swipes at the Monkees' synthetic origins. *Time*, for instance, hailed the show as "bright, unaffected and zany" only to conclude it was a "half-hour steal of the Beatles." *Newsweek* wrote that the show was "fresh stuff for TV" but then countered that the Monkees were "direct videological descendants of the Beatles" and that "television is a medium that thrives on thievery."

Raybert knew in advance that the "plastic" issue was their Achilles heel. "It was a chink," Schneider says. "It was something they could attack." Now that the show was a critical success, the producers braced themselves for the inevitable backlash. Their strategy was to stall all efforts of the press by forbidding any interviews with the Monkees — a misbegotten policy that would only exacerbate the tensions. Meanwhile, every plastic invective that the pundits could conjure was being hurled at the defenseless Monkees. But the one that stuck was the comparison to the Beatles and "A Hard Day's Night." Years later, Jim Frawley addressed this issue: "The Beatles humor was much more English, really, it was subtle and drier. Ours was much more American — it was bombastic and slapstick. We were more inspired by the Marx Brothers whereas Lester's style with the Beatles was inspired by the 'Goon Show' in England."

Whatever the source of inspiration, the Monkees' debut episode, "The Royal Flush," set an irreverent tone that would carry throughout the run of the series. The plot, concerning the Dutchess of Harmonica and her evil Uncle Otto, was almost incidental to the action — as was the case in many of the episodes. It was the cumulative effect that mattered. Unlike standard sitcom fare, "The Monkees" did not condescend to its audience. The music was rock 'n' roll, the fashions were mod, the hair was long and the jargon (reportedly checked out first by Schneider's eight year-old son Jeffrie) was right on. For the first time there were no sage parental figures or doddy old schoolmasters. But underneath the zaniness, "The Monkees" show stood for the most important catch-phrase of the era: freedom.

"Most TV is like dope," Dolenz told *Seventeen* magazine. "It's just there to put people into a state where they'll believe anything anybody says — like the announcer of the six o'clock news. Our show gives you the idea of being an individual. That's what we represent to the kids: an effort to be an individual, an attempt to find your own personality."

Instead of the rarified homespun corn of "Petticoat Junction," "The Monkees" show offered a reasonable facsimile of teenage life. What effect this had on Billy-Joe and Bobby-Jeanne McDonald from Wheatfield, USA is difficult to gauge. The effect on television, in general, was easier to measure. No longer the static, grey medium of times past, network television could now take more chances with the greening populace of America. Within a few years, adults would get their own zany show replete with "groovy" music and "far out" visual trickery — it was called "Laugh-In" and, not surprisingly, it was also on NBC.

"The Royal Flush," which later copped Emmy Awards for Outstanding Comedy Series and Direction (Frawley), was chock full of ingenuity and innovation. The masterstroke, however, was

Long hair, groovy jargon and rock 'n' roll invade the living rooms of America. "Progress can turn up in the strangest places," claimed the N.Y. Times. (From the collection of Maggie McManus)

the candid, off-stage interviews conducted with the Monkees. These last-minute tags, most of which were excised from syndicated reruns, became a signature of the early episodes almost by accident. "The reason, curiously enough, was that the first show was too long," Frawley explains, "so we edited and edited until we got it down to a minute and a half under length. And rather than lay in a minute and a half of film after we had toiled to get it down to length, we just did an experiment, which was to sit the four boys in director's chairs on the set and ask them questions. It turned out they were very amusing in their responses and it became a very warm, real part of the show."

Judging from his past experience with the pilot episode, Rafelson had learned his lesson well: audience identification was the key to the Monkees' success. The fact that the boys were allowed to retain their real names on the show was by no means an accident — it was a calculated ploy to further establish the bonds of identification. The off-stage interviews added another element of realism to the fanciful plotlines of the show. "They talked directly to the audience," Rafelson says, "They sat there unmasked, if you will, and addressed the common concerns of their audience. As a consequence, people felt they knew the Monkees."

The payoff, of course, was measured in more concrete terms by corporate executives, who viewed the Monkees venture in a somewhat different philosophical light. Record sales were their yardstick and by every measurement they stood to cash in their chips. "Last Train To Clarksville," which had been selling at a steady clip prior to the show's debut, now took a skyward leap up the charts. For NBC and the show's sponsors, Kelloggs and Yardley Cosmetics, the financial dividends came none too soon. Reservations over Raybert's unorthodox approach to business had been simmering since the very start. "I don't think anybody was too thrilled about it," Schneider recalls. "I mean, the network was never too thrilled about it, except that it worked. Who's going to argue with that? They were counting the money. At that point, as long as nobody did anything egregiously wrong, they just stayed away."

Remarkably, almost all of those involved with the show were newcomers to network television — Rafelson and Schneider were new to producing, Frawley was new to directing, and the rag-tag staff of writers were, with the exception of Dee Caruso and Gerald Gardner (formerly of "Get Smart"), all new to the medium. "There was a freewheeling madness in the office," Rafelson recalls. "We were just whaling and gunning — that's the way the show evolved."

If any one person set the tone of nonconformity, it was Rafelson himself. On the first shoot of the series in June, '66, Rafelson took cast and crew to Malibu Canyon where several locations, including a farm, had been scouted in advance for an episode entitled "A Gift Horse." When the long procession of truck and vans finally arrived at the farm with all the equipment, however, all Rafelson found was a locked gate and no farmer. Barely keeping his anger in check, Rafelson suggested to a Screen Gems official that they knock over the gate now and worry later. The official ("a typical bureaucrat," according to Rafelson) replied that such an act could not be permitted without Screen Gems' seal of approval. "So I sent him to look for the farmer," Rafelson recounts. "Then I took the first truck and I rammed the gate, broke it open and we marched in. After all, to pay for a gate was going to cost $500, but it cost $10,000 an hour to shoot. Well, we proceeded to shoot the shit out of the day and that set a pattern for leaving us alone."

Once the cash flow began to overrun the banks of their corporate backers, Rafelson and Schneider were, in essence, free to go wild. Monkeemania was no longer impending — it had arrived on a big red carpet. The fleet-footed ranks of those in the business of hucksterism stood and took notice of the latest Big Thing. The signs of success were everywhere. Even the cloistered Monkees themselves began to experience the ferment of the moment. A radio promotion, in which the boys and their fans would ride a train together to Capistrano, á la "Last Train To Capistrano," turned into a mob scene, with thousands of clutching, screaming teenyboppers giving the four Monkees their first taste of celebrity.

Following hot on the heels of "Clarksville" was the eponymously-entitled debut album, "The Monkees." Considering the last-minute haggling in the studio, the album is much better than one might expect. Despite a pancake-thin production from Boyce and Hart, "The Monkees" is, overall, a pleasant, if unchallenging, effort. Stand-out cuts include Goffin/King's "Take A Giant Step," Nesmith's "Papa Gene's Blues" and the novelty classic, "Gonna Buy Me A Dog," replete with the spontaneous studio tomfoolery of Dolenz and Jones. Best of all, there is nary a song reminiscent of the Beatles, although the album cover was a direct rip of the Beatles' balcony pose on "Please Please Me."

All in all, the debut album is more of a testament to the pop instincts of Kirshner and his cronies than it is the Monkees, who merely provided vocal tracks. Of all the Monkees, only Nesmith managed to wrangle any artistic leeway within the well-defined lines of authority. Even on his two self-produced originals, "Papa Gene's Blues" and "Sweet Young Thing," Nesmith was relegated to non-musical status due to Kirshner's strict vocals-only policy towards the Monkees.

Oblivious to the origins of the music, the public began buying the debut album faster than they had "Meet the Beatles," the first stateside release from John, Paul, George and Ringo. In short order it topped the charts at number one, where it would remain for thirteen straight weeks, setting a record that would stand for seventeen years until the 1983 debut of Men At Work. Overall, 3,200,000 copies would be cleared in less than three months, a remarkable sum considering the instant alchemic origins of the group.

"Clarksville," too, hit number one on November 5, knocking off "96 Tears" by ? And The Mysterians. The single sold well enough to clock in as the sixth most popular song of 1966. By now the hysteria had grown in such proportions that one L.A. radio station played a Monkees cut every 15 minutes for an entire month. NBC similarly found itself inundated by the 50,000 fan letters that poured in every week. Merchandise was moving faster than it could be shipped out.

Equalling the force of teenage consumption was the opposing force of negative media, which began rolling as a bandwagon, but had now become a steamroller. Suspicion that the Monkees did not perform on their records had risen from vague rumor to full-blown controversy. Worst of all, it was true. Inquisitive reporters who found themselves stymied by Raybert were none too generous in return. The anti-rock press brigades, always in search of a turkey to roast, saw an easy target in the Monkees. Secluded in their hamlets, the boys began to suffer the slings and arrows of their outrageous fortune.

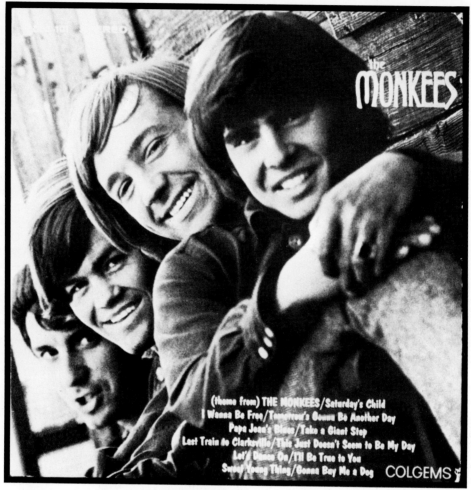

The Monkees' debut album. Notice the misspelling of "Papa Gene's Blues". (Photo reproduction by Linda S. Johnson)

Clearly, a move had to be made and fast — the Monkees had to prove their musical prowess in front of a live audience. This was no easy task. First of all, they had never played as a band before. Secondly, they were already spending seventy hours a week filming the series. Finally, they were scared witless. So they commenced rehearsals, working furiously into the night and on weekends, knowing they would have to live up to the considerable hype that preceeded them. This would be the final and most pressure-packed test of all. "Regardless of how successful the records were," explains Schneider, "if they couldn't be good onstage, no one was going to see them. Word gets around awfully fast. It's awfully hard to be number one act in the world and you've never worked in a recording studio."

Indeed, it was a phenomenon never before or since witnessed in modern music with the possible exception of Spinal Tap. Four actors playing the roles of four rock musicians on television would now have to become a real band playing in front of real people. Life had surely imitated art before, but never in such ludicrous circumstances. Consider poor Micky Dolenz, who was forced to take lessons just so he could fake playing the drums.

The test of fire was scheduled for December 3 at the Honolulu International Center Arena in Hawaii. In the great tradition of Broadway, the group would break in out of town or, as in this case, off the continent altogether. Although they were understandably nervous about their first live gig, the Monkees needn't have worried, as the pandemonium all but eclipsed their performance anyway. In fact, the ear-shattering roar that met their entrance was so overwhelming that for a split-second the group wasn't sure whether to play or flee for their lives.

The situation was best encapsulated in a concert review that later ran in the *New York Times:* "As it turned out, no one profiting from the millions being brought in on television, radio, gadgets and costume manufacture, need have worried about the investment in the Monkees. The audience protected them beautifully." Indeed, the hysteria was so great that dozens of cops were forced to wield their nightsticks agianst the crazed boppers in order to ward off a potential riot. "Fifty cops were fighting them off with clubs," Jones told *Melody Maker.* "I don't want any part of that. But I suppose they have to do it — if the girls got to us they would tear us apart."

Onstage, the Monkees ran through the debut album along with some unreleased material such as "Prithee" and "She's So Far Out She's In." Providing moral and musical support were Bobby Hart's Candy Store Prophets (a wicked pun if there ever was one), and for all their trouble they could have stayed in L.A. — hardly a single note was audible. Still, the event was a financial and critical success in more ways than one. Most importantly, the Monkees stopped accusations of their musical ineptitude dead in their tracks, at least for the time being. Their success also paved the way for more in-concert appearances. After Hawaii, the group launched a late-December tour that concentrated on mid-America, while conspiciously avoiding the media hotspots on both coasts. Conducted on the weekends between shoots, the 12-stop tour was met with enthusiasm and SRO crowds in every city from Detroit and Cincinnati to Memphis and Nashville.

Towards the end of the tour, a concert in Phoenix was filmed for a future episode of the series. Directed by Rafelson, "The Monkees On Tour" is a fascinating document (and advertisement) of the tumult surrounding the Monkees' early concerts. Although subsequent tours would be far more polished, the Phoenix concert typified the freewheeling madness of the Monkees' first appearances. The episode also included a live concert sequence that is all but muffled by screams, although the irony of Nesmith singing Willie Dixon's "You Can't Judge A Book By Its Cover" cuts through loud and clear. A nice final touch of "The Monkees On Tour" is the closing thank you to the Beatles for pointing the way.

One week after their triumph in Hawaii, the Monkees and their attendant phenomenon would scale new peaks with the double knock-out punch of "I'm A Believer"/"(I'm Not Your) Steppin' Stone." Already there had been an astounding 1,051,280 advance orders for the single, the biggest such pre-sale order since the Beatles' "Can't Buy Me Love." *Billboard's* confident expectations — "blockbuster sides that will have immediate impact" — were easily met as the single shot to number one in four short weeks. Eventually it would go on to sell a whopping 10,000,000 copies worldwide.

This time, all the hoopla was justified. The Monkees' second single release is arguably among the best double-sided hits in rock/pop history. The A-side, "I'm A Believer," was an instant bubblegum classic. Propelled by Dolenz's mock-angst vocals and one of the cheesiest organ riffs

Fifty club-wielding cops protect the boys. "If the girls got to us," said Jones, "they'd tear us apart." (Photo by Henry Diltz)

I-yi-yi-yi-I'm not your steppin' stone. Just to prove his point, Dolenz poured a Coke on Donnie's head. (Photo by Henry Diltz)

this side of the local roller rink, "I'm A Believer" quickly became the Monkees' signature song. The flip side, Boyce and Hart's "Steppin' Stone" was originally recorded by Paul Revere and the Raiders, the second time that band had mis-timed a potential hit (the first time being their lesser known version of "Louie, Louie," which lost out to the Kingsmen's garage-rock classic).

On its own merits, the Monkees' rendition of "Steppin' Stone" manager to crack the top twenty. Years later, the song lives on in the repertoire of all fledgling rock bands. Even the legendary Sex Pistols paid homage to the song on their "The Great Rock 'n' Roll Swindle" compilation. "It's kind of a phenomenon," says co-author Bobby Hart regarding "Steppin' Stone's" lasting appeal. "It's one of the first songs that every garage-rock band in the country learns to play. That's probably because it's an easy four chords." That's E-G-A-C for all you guitar heroes out there.

The fortuitous release of "I'm A Believer"/"(I'm Not Your) Steppin' Stone" pushed the Monkees into another realm altogether: superstardom. And, as a result, they wouldn't be stepping stones for very much longer. One must stop and consider how much had happened in so little time to the groups' members. Within three months, they had placed two number one singles and one number one album (with another one ready for release) on the charts, and had won kudos for their weekly T.V. series and their lucrative concert appearances.

The mania-starved pre-teens, many of whom had missed the boat on Beatlemania, began channeling their nascent hormonal urges into a compulsive consumerism. Anyone with any business acumen quickly swayed their allegiance to the Monkees. Teenzines, such as *Tiger Beat* and *16 Magazine*, swiftly replaced the Beatles' mugs for the Monkees on their covers. Those in control of the kitty began jockeying for a bigger piece of the pie. Outside parties, some of them illicit, also wanted a cut. Rafelson recalls, "the mafioso were coming into the office saying 'we're taking over Davy Jones' career and sell Davy Jones this and Davy Jones that.' You wouldn't believe some of the behind-the-scenes weirdness that went on. Muscle, there was a lot of muscle."

Needless to say, the power, the money and the glory began playing tricks on the minds of those involved. After all the disparagement in the press, the Monkees and their backers were more than willing to wallow in a little self-adulatory praise. Tommy Boyce told Rhino Records, "I felt a little embarrassed after a while knowing a song I wrote today would be number one around the world tomorrow."

While others basked in the glory of the moment, the Monkees were beginning to show signs of discontent. To begin with, each member made a mere $450 per week on the series — truly pittance compared with the overflowing coffers of their backers. To make matters worse, each received a measly 1.25% royalty on all record sales, while Kirshner took a whopping 15 percent.

Even more frustrating was the persistent deception. Due to Raybert's protective policies regarding press access, rumors, both true and false, had circulated nationwide, the most common of which attacked the Monkees' musical prowess or lack thereof. The Monkees, lacking a forum for their defense, were reduced to bowling pins, knocked down, dragged out and then mechanically set back up again. Relevance, á la the Buffalo Springfield's "For What It's Worth" was now expected from groups that previously pushed only "Fun, Fun, Fun." Those over the age of fifteen had little patience with a phenomenon that, in the eyes of the public, was nothing more than a money-making enterprise with little or nothing to say.

Thus, the Monkees, gagged and bound as they were, found themselves crushed between the proverbial rock and the hard place. Their corporate sponsors cared not a whit about this dilemma as long as the ring of the cash register did not cease. Far more damage could be done, in their minds, if one of the Monkees dared to say something topical about drugs or Vietnam. That just wouldn't wash in Wichita, so the muzzle remained intact.

Surprisingly, the reins and the whip were wielded by none other than Rafelson and Schneider, two men whose liberal credentials and integrity have rarely been in doubt. Schneider, who handled the business end of the partnership, was particularly cautious, as he later admitted: "I had a lot of desire to manage the way in which the press got a hold of them. It was like walking a tightrope all the time, because, on the one hand, we wanted to encourage the creativity of the Monkees but, at the same time, we wanted to keep it manageable so it didn't end up with a phone call that said 'you're cancelled.'

Papa's Blue Jeans? A quick-buck cash-in, pre-dating the Banana Splits. (Photo reproduction by Linda S. Johnson)

It's grrrrreat! A free Monkees record on the back of cereal boxes. Moms everywhere were somewhat less enthusiastic. (Photo reproduction by Linda S. Johnson)

"We were walking the line between industrial America, on one hand, and rebellion, on the other. What we stood for was the rebellion, but at the same time, we were dealing with the real world. I was very personally desirous of manipulating the situation so that we wouldn't get our heads chopped off."

Raybert's hands-off policy soon faced greater pressures from the ranks of the scoop-hungry press corps. In an attempt to counterbalance the weight of their demands, Raybert became overzealous in their effort to bide time. Of all their ploys, none stooped as low as the phony press releases. "Raybert wanted an atmosphere of mystique," Dolenz later told Rhino Records. "They didn't want us to do interviews, so they arranged phony press conferences where they would send in their own reporters from Screen Gems and NBC. . . and we had stock answers to all these questions, many times funny ones, just to avoid the problems. The trouble is everybody wants to make you some sort of prophet just because you're an entertainer. Already they were making comparisons between us and the Beatles."

In actuality, with the smash hit "I'm A Believer" riding the top of the charts for ten straight weeks, the Monkees *were* now outselling the Beatles. Against such stiff competition as the Stones' "Ruby Tuesday," the Beach Boys' "Good Vibrations" and the Beatles' "Penny Lane"/"Strawberry Fields Forever," the Monkees were not only holding their own, they were holding the brass ring as well.

The Monkees as individuals now had the clout they needed. Each was a household name and together they were, in the lingo of LA-LA land, "guaranteed box office." Their first collective act of power was to force Raybert's hand concerning the press issue — it was time to go public. Despite their reservations, Raybert reluctantly agreed. The first reporter to get a crack at the group was

Davy gets the scoop on his latest romance from the colorful pages of Tiger Beat. (Photo by Henry Diltz)

Judy Stone from the venerable *New York Times*. Aptly titled "The Monkees Let Down Their Hair," the article was hardly the sensational expose that Raybert feared. Part of this was due, no doubt, to the presence of Screen Gem officials, who cast a watchful eye over the proceedings. Despite the monitoring, some of the Monkees' pent-up frustrations could not be suppressed any longer. "We're advertisers," Jones candidly admitted. "We're selling a product. We're selling Monkees. It's gotta be that way."

Of all the members, Tork took the most liberties, dangling the forbidden carrot in a test of his limitations. "If you want something really visionary and mystic," he told the *Times*, "telepathy is the coming phenomenon. Nonverbal, extrasensory communication is at hand." As the blood pressure of Screen Gems officials slowly came to a boil, Tork broached the touchy topic of war. "I stand for love and peace," he explained. "To my way of thinking, they're the same thing. But the man who said 'My country, right or wrong' made a slight error in judgement. My country wrong needs my help. Well, I guess I've got myself in enough hot water."

In general, little or no damage had been done by the *Times* article, however. More reporters would now sieze their chance to confront the Monkees, who were now more than willing to confess all. The worst fears of the Monkees corporation — the truth — soon came to pass under the no-holds-barred policy of press freedom. The normally staid *Saturday Evening Post* ran the expose in January, 1967 that opened the floodgates of controversy. The article, an expertly written and researched piece of journalism by Richard Warren Lewis, is perhaps the most definitive behind-the-scenes probe of the group ever committed to paper. The scientific packaging of the Monkees is carefully and accurately dissected with revealing quotes from the four overworked, under-paid, much-maligned Monkees.

By far the most damaging revelations were the acerbic comments of an embittered Nesmith. Controversy over musical control had been slowly bubbling under since the success of "I'm A Believer." Ever since the release of the first album, Nesmith had been demanding a more significant role in the creative process. Kirshner, not wanting to rock the boat, appeased the Monkees with vague promises that never materialized. Tensions mounted further when Kirshner replaced Nesmith for Dolenz on the lead vocals of "I'm A Believer." Bad blood between Kirshner and Nesmith was by no means an isolated case. Tork, too, harboured ill-feelings as did Dolenz, who vented his frustrations by pouring a bottle of Coke on Kirshner's head in the studio.

Never a shy man when push came to shove, Nesmith saw the opportunity to take his case public. Utilizing his most ornery invective, Nesmith read the riot act: "The music has nothing to do with us," he disclosed to the *Post*. "It was totally dishonest. Do you know how debilitating it is to sit up and have to duplicate somebody else's records? That's really what we were doing."

Nesmith: "Tell the world we're synthetic because, damn it, we are." Dolenz, Tork, and Jones: "Thanks, Mike." (Photo by Henry Diltz)

"Maybe we were manufactured and put on the air strictly with a lot of hoopla," he continued later in the article. "Tell the world that we're synthetic because, damn it, we are. Tell them the Monkees were wholly man-made overnight, that millions of dollars have been poured into this thing. Tell the world we don't record our own music. But that's us they see on television. The show is really part of us. They're not seeing something invalid."

Although such a disclosure was inevitable, the Monkees were, as a peaking phenomenon, at their most vulnerable. Nesmith's revelations, which were well known within the industry, sent shockwaves through the legions of older, more discerning, fans of the group. Not surprisingly, the media vultures pounced ravenously on the raw meat. The reaction, in the public domain, was swift and profound. All the allegations and innuendo that had been passed on as rumor now came to the fore. The Monkees became the counterculture's favorite whipping boys.

Within the ranks of the group, reportedly no one was too thrilled by Nesmith's display of brute honesty and brazen candor. The Texas vigilantism of Nesmith clashed with the laissez faire attitude of Jones and Dolenz, who considered themselves actors first, performers second and musicians a distant third. Tork, on the other hand, was a former folkie with idealistic intentions that were in accord with Nesmith's desires. Thus, the crew quickly split into two divergent camps regarding their artistic aspirations.

Nesmith and Tork's vexations are easily understandable in light of Dolenz and Jones' lion's share of the lead vocals. "From Kirshner's point of view, Davy and Micky were the commercial elements in selling records and Nesmith and Tork were inconsequential," Schneider contends. "I think Michael and Peter were equally pained about their roles, although Michael may have been a little more aggressive than Peter."

Tork, who had to play the fourth banana on the series, was now near the end of his rope. "I was mortified that the records were being made without me. I felt humiliated, shunned and slighted," he recalled years after. "The worst thing was that nobody seemed to notice. I would scream and yell and rave and they would scratch their heads. Absolute incomprehension."

With Tork in the fold, Nesmith needed to enlist the support of the skeptical Dolenz and Jones — the top two Monkees in terms of popularity — in joining their crusade. Dolenz later expressed his attitude in an interview with Rhino Records: "The drums to me were more or less a prop for a long time. To Mike and Peter, however, the music mattered most. So every time they had to pander or compromise their music it really affected them deeply."

The breaking point for all four Monkees occured on January 15, 1967 in Cleveland, Ohio, where the group was scheduled to perform that night. While browsing through a record store, the group found a copy of an album they had neither seen nor heard before — "More Of The Monkees." When they finally got the opportunity to listen, they did not enjoy what they heard. Thrown together in haphazard fashion, "More Of The Monkees" would only add fuel to the fire concerning the Monkees' supposed musical ineptitude. The boys were livid. "I regard the 'More Monkees' album as probably the worst album in the history of the world, "Nesmith growled to *Hit Parader.*

Although such a drastic appraisal is certainly exaggerated, "More Of The Monkees" did deliver precious few inspirational moments beyond the inclusion of "I'm A Believer" and "Steppin' Stone." Boyce and Hart's headbanger, "She," and the inspired lunacy of "Your Auntie Grizelda" were passable, but hardly earthshaking. Overall, there was a disjointed, unsatisfying feel to the album, attributable in no small measure to nine separate producers (which must be a record of some sort) who worked on the different tracks. Kirshner stuck to the hard and fast rule that top-flight studio professionals could outperform the real band every time. The results of this policy were best illustrated by Nesmith's sprightly rocker "Mary Mary." Instead of allowing Nesmith to handle the instrumental end of his own composition, Glen Campbell was recruited for lead guitar. What Kirshner did not realize, however, was the bloodless quality that such policies insured. For all their flawless technique, studio musicians could never quite capture the fire of the true originals. As a result, the Monkees sounded pale and flat.

Most galling of all, though, were the self-serving liner notes on the back cover of "More Of The Monkees," written by none other than the Golden Ear himself. In what turned out to be an amazing display of megalomania, Kirshner listed the names of his prized staff of songwriters before the individual Monkees were even mentioned. "The back liner notes were Don Kirshner congratulating all his boys for the wonderful work they'd done, and oh yes, this record is by the Monkees. It was very hard to take," Tork told *Goldmine* years later. If that wasn't enough, the front cover photo was yet another cop of the Beatles and the psychedelic motif employed on "Rubber Soul."

Needless to say, the Monkees were infuriated about the crass, commercial approach of the entire album. Kirshner had betrayed the group by going strictly MOR (read: MOR money). "He was pure vanilla," Schneider says of Kirshner, "and they were not, nor were we." The rift between Kirshner and his "clones" was now a chasm. Ramifications were not far away.

Ironically, but then again hardly surprising, "More Of The Monkees" became the best-selling Monkees album of all time. Some 5,000,000 discs eventually sold as the album rode the crest of the charts for a phenomenal eighteen weeks. For several months in early '67, both Monkees albums would dominate the charts at the two highest positions, a feat matched only by the Beatles.

The year 1967 had barely arrived and the tide of Monkeemania showed no signs of ebbing. Merchandising — in the form of lunch pails, wool hats and bubblegum cards — began to have residual effect upon the rest of the entertainment industry. The news that had the bigwigs from RCA, NBC and Screen Gems smiling from coast to coast was reported by Billboard: "Their simple, appealing zaniness has snowballed. . . into the biggest and fastest selling commodity since the Beatles. Their Monkees brand of talent has innoculated the market with a welcome splash of high sales, whose ripples extend as far as soaring circulations for fan and music consumer publications. The Monkees rapid ascent to international fame and fortune marks another major phase in the renaissance of American talent in the world's hit parades so long dominated by Liverpool and then London."

England, in fact, was in the throes of its own Monkeemania by this time. Without video exposure, "Clarksville" had initially bombed on the British charts. In January '67, however, the

In a rare moment, both Nesmith and Tork enjoy the rollercoaster ride. Notice the security guards in the background. (Photo by Henry Diltz)

Monkeemaniacs greet their heroes at the airport. Dig those wigged-out frames. (Photo by Henry Diltz)

A British accent was worth its weight in gold. In London, another David Jones was forced to change his name to Bowie. (Photo by Henry Diltz)

show reached the shores simultaneous to the release of "I'm A Believer," which became an instantaneous number one smash.

Within a few short weeks, the trend-conscious Brits had elevated the Monkees to the status of the Holy Trinity plus one. Never before had an American act dominated the aesthetic sensibilities of the British with such wide-ranging conviction. "In something under a week," *Variety* reported, "the act has been accorded attention surpassed only by Soviet Premier Alexei Kosygin's visit to the U.K." Once again, the Monkees had rejuvenated an entire nation's entertainment industry. "Where there was comparative peace and slow business," wrote *Variety,* "all is hipped up and the wax industry is once more humming."

In a clever bit of marketing strategy, Dolenz, Jones, and Nesmith arrived overseas separately to promote the show. Naturally, native Englander Davy's arrival caused the biggest stir of all. The near riot that met Jones at Heathrow airport was later reported by the stuffy *London Times* with an air of detached bemusement:

> Tempers began to fray as the hysterical girls waving banners and balloons started to chant, "We want Davy." Screaming teenagers tore through the terminal building to try to catch sight of Jones. Others staged a sit-down protest on the roadway leading to the tarmac. Inside, police and airport staff struggled to get incoming passengers through the arrival doors which buckled under the weight of the girls pressing against them...
>
> Long after Jones had been driven out of the airport by a backroad, the teenagers refused to believe he had left. They blocked the airport staircases and drowned flight announcements by repeatedly chanting, "We want Davy."
>
> Five hours later more than 200 were still running wild through the building.
> Eventually police regained control by threatening to turn the fire hoses on them.

Incidentally, Jones' popularity by this time was so overwhelming that another young British singer named David Jones was forced to change his name to David Bowie.

Much like America, England met the Monkees with equal parts hysteria and equal parts wrath. The British had long considered rock music in more intellectual terms than their Yankee counterparts. *Melody Maker,* the dean of the British rock journals at the time, reported the resulting schisms within the music community: "Oh, the bitchiness! Oh, the arguments! Oh, the rows! It's amazing how pop can still cause furor and uproar from one side of the Atlantic to the other. A mighty thunder of sledgehammers filling the air as the knockers get to grips with their latest self-appointed task — demolitioning the Monkees."

In response to the controversy, *Melody Maker* ran an open debate in their pages between the equally vocal supporters and detractors of the Monkees. Music industry insiders such as Eric Burdon of the blues-purist Animals were asked their opinion of this latest craze. Burdon, for one, rose in defense of the Monkees. "They make very good records," he told *Melody Maker* "and I can't understand how people get upset about them. You've got to make up your minds whether a group is a record production group or one that makes live appearances. For example, I like to hear a Phil Spector record and I don't worry if it's the Ronettes or Ike and Tina Turner... I like the Monkees record as a good record, no matter how people scream. So somebody made record and they don't play, so what? Just enjoy the record."

Arriving in the midst of this fray was Micky Dolenz, who towed a similar line as Burdon had in his defense to *Melody Maker:* "What's all the fuss about? Nobody criticizes Sonny and Cher for not playing on their records, or Sinatra for not playing all those 21 strings."

Back in the States, more trouble was stirring for the beleaguered creators of the group. The first of several lawsuits involving both Raybert and the Monkees had been filed in late January by David Yarnell and David Gordon, who claimed to have submitted the original idea for the show, entitled "Liverpool, USA," to Screen Gems in 1964. Later settled out of court for an undisclosed sum, such suits were haunting reminders of how fragile the house-of-cards foundations of the project actually were.

Pressures were also mounting from the higher-ups at RCA to follow up on the resounding success of "I'm A Believer." Unlike today's practices, groups during the mid-Sixties rarely waited more than three or four months between releasing new vinyl. The Monkees, however, had nothing in the cans due to the extraordinary pace of their lives, which now included touring, filming and recording. In addition, their musical direction was truly at a crossroads. Stung by criticism and disillusioned by the record-making machinery, the group's confidence was at an all-time low, though touring had buoyed their spirits considerably. Now that the four Monkees had proven to themselves that they could perform in front of a live audience, they wanted a crack at recording their own songs.

With two number one albums and two number one singles under their belts, the boys finally agreed on one thing — to chop off the Golden Ear.

As usual, Nesmith took the initiative. Scouring the clubs for a producer, Nesmith met up with Chip Douglas at the Whiskey A Go-Go. Douglas, who had formerly been a member of the seminal Modern Folk Quartet, was now playing bass with the Turtles, whose "Happy Together" was bubbling up the charts. After the Turtles gig, Nesmith approached Douglas point-blank and offered him the job. Years later, Douglas remembers the conversation, "I said, 'I never produced a record in my life.' I had no idea about highs and lows and volumes and levels. And he said, 'that's alright, I'll teach you everything you need to know.' "

The probability of this arrangement coming to pass was highly unlikely under the thumb of Kirshner and company. Nesmith's revelations in the *Saturday Evening Post*, which were widely circulated by now, had forced a summit meeting, however. Judgement Day had arrived. The showdown was set for the Beverly Hills Hotel where the superpowers, Monkees #1 and Monkees #2, would meet. With Douglas in tow, the four boys (Monkees #2) met Kirshner (Monkee #1) in his swank $150-a-day suite. Also there were Kirshner's corporate henchmen, Lester Sill and Herb Moelis. Conspicious in their absence were Rafelson and Schneider, who wisely stayed away.

The tension-filled confrontation started off in perverse fashion as Kirshner made a presentation of gold records for the "More of the Monkees" album. Now it would be that much more difficult for the Monkees to plead their case. Undaunted, Nesmith came forward with a list of demands — they wanted to play their own music, choose their own music and have Douglas produce the whole thing. Kirshner could oversee, but not dictate, from now on.

Douglas remembers the uneasiness of the scene: "I was very awed by the whole thing. Suddenly, here I was in the driver's seat. It was very scary looking back on it. I felt like a little shrimp amongst all these lobsters." Douglas' presence turned out to be crucial, however, as Kirshner countered the Monkees' demands by handing the group four new demo tapes he had already assembled, one of which was "Sugar Sugar" (later, of course, a monster hit for the Archies). "I'm glad I was in there at the time," Douglas says. "I probably saved the Monkees from having to do some *real* bubblegum."

The conflict basically centered on the two equally stubborn antagonists, Kirshner and Nesmith. When Kirshner launched into a vainglorious sermon on the realities of the music business, Nesmith heatedly replied, "Donnie, we could sing 'Happy Birthday' with a beat and it would sell a million records." Kirshner still refused to budge. Emotions were now barely under check as the

*"That could have been your face!" Nesmith may have won the battle,
but Kirshner got the "Sugar, Sugar".*

confrontation took an ugly turn. Nesmith issued an ultimatum: either the Monkees got musical control or he quit. Herb Moelis, responding to the threat, commented to Nesmith that he had better read his contract first. Nesmith answered by ramming his fist through the hotel wall and snarling to Moelis, "that could have been your face," before storming out of the room.

Nesmith later recalled the essence of his argument. "Essentially the big collision I had with Don Kirshner was this: he kept saying, 'you can't make the music, it would be no good, it won't be a hit.' And I was saying, 'hey, the music is not a hit because somebody wonderful is making it, the music is a hit because of the television show. So, at least let us put out music that is closer to our personas, closer to who were are artistically, so that we don't have to walk around and have people throwing eggs at us,' which they were."

The entire confrontation was later documented in *TV Guide,* in an article entitled "The Great Revolt of '67." Kirshner gave a somewhat different interpretation of the event, however, in *The Making of Superstars:* "The Monkees were very temperamental guys. I had given them royalty checks for over a million dollars at a time — kids who previously had nothing. After the first two hits, Mike said he didn't like the way the records had been produced. I was out at the Beverly Hills Hotel with my wife and mother-in-law and friend, Herb Moelis, and we were all pretty happy, what with the success of the Monkees. And, in front of everybody, Mike gave me a hard time and proceeded to put his fist through the wall."

The lines were now clearly drawn — it was the Monkees versus Kirshner and something had to give. Ultimately, this decision rested in the hands of Raybert, who somehow managed to strike an accord. The Monkees would go into the recording studio and prove themselves. In the end, the support of Schneider had been the Monkees' trump card. "Another guy would have said, 'I can't let you do it boys, Kirshner would take us to court,' " Tork says of Schneider, "but Bert doesn't mind a fight. He won't be threatened or bludgeoned. If he wants to do it, he'll go ahead and do it. And he wanted us to do it. That's what I love about Bert — he didn't goad us, but he certainly didn't deny us the effort."

Schneider bears out Tork's testimonial by saying, "I was totally in accord with their desires as long as it wasn't going to make it a flop. If it was going to make everything a flop, then there was no point to it, it was just self-destructive. I was trying to run a middle course between eventually getting to where they wanted to go and Kirshner's approach, which was 'don't let them do anything.'"

Wasting no time, the four Monkees eagerly entered the studios with Douglas at the production controls. Each Monkee assumed a separate musical role with Tork on keyboards, Nesmith on guitar, Dolenz on the drums and Jones on percussion. Douglas chipped in on bass. Together, the quintet cut two songs intended for the next single release — Bill Martin's "I'm Just One Of Your Toys" and Nesmith's "The Girl I Knew Somewhere."

Kirshner, meanwhile, carried on as if nothing had ever happened. In his mind, he didn't need the Monkees, he just needed their voices. Surreptitiously, he coaxed Jones into the studio to cut more tracks, including Jeff Barry's "She Hangs Out" and two by Neil Diamond — "Love To Love" and "A Little Bit Me, A Little Bit You." Of these three songs, only the unreleased "Love To Love" (which was later included on Rhino's invaluable "Monkee Business" compilation) had any punch, in this case owing to one of the hottest guitar tracks on Monkees vinyl. Unfortunately, Diamond's other cut was no gem. Sounding suspiciously like his previous hit, "Cherry Cherry," "A Little Bit Me, A Little Bit You" is a little bit limp. In fact, if one listens closely, it is possible to detect the

So you wanna be a rock'n'roll star? Get a TV show, kid. (Photo by Henry Diltz)

dulcet tones of Diamond himself on the backing track. Although this observation shatters the widely held belief that the Monkees provided all the vocals on every cut, apparently such a practice was not uncommon. "On most of the records I did with the Monkees," Kirshner told *The Making of Superstars* in typical exaggerated fashion, "Carole King and Neil Diamond would sing background."

Kirshner had good reason to keep plugging away, considering his 15% royalty on every Monkees record. With his infallible, but artistically bankrupt, method of fabricating records, Kirshner had a virtual bonanza in his midst. And, yet, what he desperately needed now was to upstage the Monkees, who were swiftly maneuvering themselves into Kirshner's territory. "There was a little bit of overlap," Douglas remembers about this period of time. "It was kind of tense for a while. Kirshner was having them do one thing while I was trying to get them to do another."

With the imminent release of the Monkees' own single, Kirshner needed a pretext to delay the inevitable. Eventually, he found such an excuse — he could enforce Screen Gems' strict policies regarding publishing rights to thwart the release of "I'm Just One Of Your Toys," a song with an outside copyright. Since all Colgem releases needed the Screen Gems publishing imprimatur, the new single would have to be shelved indefinitely. In fact, "I'm Just One Of Your Toys" remains the great lost Monkees song, never having gone beyond an acetate pressing.

In an act of sheer bravado, Kirshner seized the opportunity to release a new single, "A Little Bit Me, A Little Bit You"/"She Hangs Out" without the group's consent. This calculated ploy would prove to be Kirshner's fatal error. Obviously, the audacity of such a move was a complete affront to the Monkees and Raybert, both of whom cried foul. Before it could hit the record stores, the single was yanked (although it was released in Canada) and Kirshner was promptly and unceremoniously dumped as musical supervisor of the Monkees.

Still reeling from Kirshner's stunning departure, Colgems called up Lester Sill and Emil Viola to replace the Golden Ear. Their first act as Colgems co-chiefs was to re-release the withdrawn single with Nesmith's "The Girl I Knew Somewhere" on the B-side. The public, ignorant of this bitter behind-the-scenes struggle, sent "A Little Bit Me, A Little Bit You" right up to the Top Five, where it peaked at number two. The flip side — the first Monkees-penned *and* performed compositon on vinyl — also fared respectably, charting as high as thirty-nine.

A closer look at the two sides of the single reveals the philosophical polarity between Kirshner and the Monkees. The A-side, as discussed previously, lacks the punch of Diamond's previous hit, "I'm A Believer." It's lackluster feel is damning evidence of Kirshner's decline. On the other hand, the B-side, Nesmith's "The Girl I Knew Somewhere" is a resounding triumph. A breezy, up-tempo number, "The Girl I Knew Somewhere" highlights the individual Monkees' musical strengths from Dolenz's wistful vocals and Tork's adept keyboards to Nesmith's songwriting chops. Although never released on an album (it is available on several greatest hits packages), "The Girl I Knew Somewhere" is essential listening not only for its musical merits but for its historical import as well.

The Monkees organization had not heard the last of Kirshner, however. On February 27, 1967, Kirshner filed suit in federal court against Columbia/Screen Gems to the tune of $35,500,000. Accusing them of conspiracy and breach of contract, Kirshner hired the hottest lawyer in the land, Edward Bennet Williams, to plead his case. Within weeks, Columbia/Screen Gems would file countercharges in federal court, issuing a statement that claimed, "Kirshner caused or permitted to be issued self-adulatory publicity which was demeaning to the Monkees." Other charges included the unauthorizied release of the the third single and an accusation that Kirshner had withheld master tapes in a publishing royalty dispute with Raybert prior to the show's debut.

Although the case made a big splash in the trade papers, it was quietly settled out of court many months later. Kirshner alleges that he "got the biggest settlement in the history of Columbia Pictures," in *The Making Of Superstars*. "It was such a large settlement that I was not allowed to disclose the amount at the time."

As the dust from the court dispute settled, the debate raged on as to Kirshner's role in the Monkees' success. There was no doubt that Kirshner had indeed usurped his authority by releasing the third single without authorization. The publicity Kirshner drew to himself was far more damaging to the group's enduring image, however. Even today, people still believe that Kirshner actually created the group, despite the fact that he came into the project well after the pilot. Ironically, Kirshner's public displays shattered the very myth that had sold so many records — that the Monkees were a real group. This seemingly self-destructive policy is what ultimately led to Kirshner's demise. "My feeling was fine," Rafelson says of Kirshner's role, "just don't take the credit for it because you'll eliminate half your audience — authenticity, integrity and a certain kind of pop truth being the slogans of the day."

Schneider, who dealt more directly with Kirshner than Rafelson, is also less forgiving in his

*Tork signs a magazine for the fuzz. Later, they would throw the book at **him**. (Photo by Henry Diltz)*

assessment: "The Monkees were much more oppressed by Kirshner's ego and his grabbing of all the credit in the papers than the rest of us. I didn't give a shit what he said, except that it damaged the group. My attitude was, 'this was all very successful so let's not rock the boat,' but Kirshner had an ego that transcended everything else. As a matter of fact, the press issue was probably magnified a hundred times over because of Kirshner. He wanted everybody thinking, 'hey, he's doing all this, not them.' In the end, it was very self-destructive because it heightened the whole press issue and it made them feel lousy. They were the butts of the attack, not Kirshner, not me, not Bob."

Kirshner, it seems, never did assimilate the factors behind his dismissal. "They had just resigned me to a ten-year deal and probably felt threatened by my earning so much," he reported to *The Making of Superstars.* "So, instead of being a mensch and calling me in and settling it by renegotiating my contract which I would be happy to do. . . they fired me. Just like that."

In retrospect, Kirshner had gone from hero to goat in a remarkably short time. Only a few months prior to their clash at the Beverly Hills Hotel, the four Monkees had given Kirshner a 48 x 48 photograph of themselves with an inscription that read: "To the man who made it all possible." Indeed, without the groundwork Kirshner had laid, it is doubtful whether the Monkees would have ever evolved as a musical entity. By establishing the Monkee's recognition factor far beyond anyone's expectations, the boys now had the clout to go at it alone. Kirshner had, in fact, pulled off one of the greatest coups in rock history. With the inestimable power of television behind him, Kirshner had taken a group that, in reality, did not exist and created for them two million-selling albums and three gold singles.

The legacy of Kirshner's contributions were felt throughout the remaining years of the Monkees, who begrudgingly gave credit where it was due. "He had a tremendous sense for what was commercial," Schneider admits, "and was able to take his producers and get the best out of them or send them back in to add things. What he did was very significant. Songs like 'I'm A Believer' were his doings — it was his connection to Jeff Barry, Neil Diamond and his East Coast people."

Although the Monkees fought impassionately to free themselves of Kirshner's stranglehold, not everyone, including Bobby Hart, is convinced that their freedom paid off. "At that point their musical career started to decline," Hart says of Kirshner's departure, "because they didn't take advantage of the high-caliber professionals they had at their disposal. They started using their friends and their songs instead. They could have had the same kind of run the Beatles had if they had fallen into the machinery and done it the way it was planned — hire all the best in every category to take care of everything, the publicity, the sponsors, the television and the live shows."

The sweet taste of revenge — two Emmy awards. Take that, Gilligan! (From the collection of Michael Dolenz)

Tork counters such logic, however, with an altogether different scenario of what-might-have-been-if-only. "What Donnie didn't know," Tork asserts, "was that he could have gone right on being the same guy he was, doing the same things he did, having the same guys be our producers. All we wanted to do was be the musicians in the chairs. But for some reason, and to this day I don't know what it was, he saw that as a challenge."

Even with Kirshner out of their way, the Monkees' troubles were far from over. The possibility that Jones might be drafted by the U.S. Army (he was considered a tax-paying U.S. citizen) hung ominously in the air in the spring of '67. Little girls everywhere said a special prayer for their beloved Davy, who might soon be a Monkee in the jungles of Southeast Asia. Fortunately, Jones managed to dodge the call-up due to the fact that he was the sole financial support for his dear dad in England.

In spite of the controversy that had shadowed the group, the Monkees' popularity had not abated. *Variety,* the showbiz bible, reported that "The Monkees" show had been renewed for a second season. "The kids have done nice enough," they wrote, "to insure at least another semester of Beatles-type film fun, and that might be all the producers need to clinch Ft. Knox honors for a long time to come."

Indeed, with the two Monkees albums clocking in at the number one position for 31 straight weeks, the stakes were higher than ever. While the high rolling corporate backers split their booty, the Monkees played on, empty-handed by comparison. In addition to their $450-a-week stipend and their paltry 1.25% royalty on the records, the Monkees were supposed to receive 10% of the merchandising (years later Dolenz and Jones would sue for funds they allegedly never obtained) and 30% of the concert gate. This financial disparity did not elude the group's members, who were beginning to ferment a keener sense of propriety and caution in their business dealings. "When you start to grow and get more successful," Jones explains, "all of a sudden you want to get out of the stock room, stop sharpening the pencils and making the coffee and you want to start getting a little more involved in the business end of it."

Channeling their latent resentment, the Monkees got set to record a new album entitled "Headquarters." This time they would play the instruments and pick the songs. Despite their popularity — they were now the world's top-selling act — the Monkees knew they had a great hurdle to leap. In order to win the hearts of skeptical fans, the Monkees would have to compete with the likes of the Beatles and the Stones. The Monkees, however, had one hard-to-ignore handicap: their image. "The Beatles, the Rolling Stones, the Beach Boys — they own themselves," Jones explained to *Seventeen.* "We don't. It's not as bad as it was in the beginning, but we're still mechanical toys, told to go here, do that, don't talk about the war in Vietnam or whatever. I wouldn't mind so much if I were working in a factory at a loom or something, but this is different."

As if to compensate for their vacuous image, the Monkees were now less guarded in their interviews. More than any one thing, the group desired that intangible about which Otis and Aretha had sung: R-E-S-P-E-C-T, just a little bit. The public could be forgiven for their media-fueled animosity, but those in the entertainment industry who took pleasure in ridiculing the group could not. After all, the Monkees and their creators had not worked miracles — they had merely exploited an idea that seemed, in retrospect, so obvious. The result of their opportunism was jealousy, plain and simple. Industry insiders, envious of the overnight success of the project, cast a jaundiced eye on every move that the Monkees made. For the group, it was a no-win situation.

Retribution lurked just around the corner, however. The recognition the Monkees so desperately sought from their peers would be obtained at the Emmy Awards. On June 5, 1967, "The Monkees" show copped top honors for Outstanding Comedy Achievement for the debut episode, "Royal Flush." After all the abuse they had weathered, the Monkees finally tasted the fine wine of sweet revenge.

The award ceremony marked a significant turning point in the history of the Monkees. Now an established entity, they would no longer worry about the consequences of their actions. They were free.

And with the "Summer of Love" approaching, they enjoyed the fruits of their liberation. None other than Timothy Leary, the acid guru of flower power, bestowed his hallowed praise upon the group. On his plane of perpetually higher consciousness, Leary was able to look past the wall of prejudice that had imprisoned the Monkees. In fact, he was one of the few hippies ever to see the light. In his book, *The Politics of Ecstasy,* Leary wrote:[3]

The average Mom and Dad, sitting gently in front of the television set, are unaware of the complex guerrilla skirmishes raging in the streets outside the door between the kids and the menopausal society. The reflex instinct of distrust and suspicion of the establishment, the underground — Negroes, Mexicans, artists, Puerto Ricans, hippies, kids.

The youngsters see it. Skillful and experienced at handling the media and psychedelic drugs (on which they were nursed), they know how to react. Take, for example, the classic case of the Monkees.

Hollywood executives decide to invent and market an American version of the Beatles — the early, preprophetic, cute, yeh-yeh Beatles. Got it? They audition a hallfull of candidates and type-cast four cute kids. Hire some songwriters. Wire up the Hooper-rating computer. What do the screaming teeny-boppers want? Crank out the product and promote it. Feed the great consumer monster what it thinks it wants, plastic, syrupy, tasty, marshmallow-filled, chocolate-coated, Saran-wrapped, and sell it. No controversy, no protest. No thinking strange, unique thoughts. No offending Mom and Dad and the advertisers. Make it silly, sun-tanned, grinning ABC-TV.

And what happened? The same thing that happened to the Beatles. The four young Monkees weren't fooled for a moment. They went along with the system but didn't buy it. Like all the beautiful songs of the new age — Peter Fonda and Robert Walker and young John Barrymore and young Steinbeck and the wise young Hitchcocks — the Monkees use the new energies to sing the new songs and pass on the new message.

The Monkees' television show, for example. Oh, you thought that was silly teen-age entertainment? Don't be fooled. While it lasted, it was a classic Sufi put-on. An early-Christian electronic satire. A mystic-magic show. A jolly Buddha laugh at hypocrisy. At early evening kiddie-time on Monday the Monkees would rush through a parody drama, burlesquing the very shows that glue Mom and Dad to the set during prime time. Spoofing the movies and violence and the down-heavy-conflict-emotion themes that fascinate the middle-aged.

And woven into the fast-moving psychedelic stream of action were the prophetic, holy, challenging words. Micky was rapping quickly, dropping literary names, making scholarly references; then the sudden psychedelic switch of the reality channel. He looked straight at the camera, right into your living room, and up-leveled the comedy by saying: "Pretty good talking for a long-haired wierdo, huh, Mr. and Mrs. America?" And then-zap. Flash. Back to the innocuous comedy.

Or, in a spy drama, Micky warned Peter: "Why this involves the responsibility for blowing up the entire world!"

Peter, confidentially: "I'll take that responsibility!"

And Micky, with a glance at the camera, said, "Wow! With a little more ego he'll be ready to run for President."

Why, it all happened so fast, LBJ, you didn't ever see it.

THE SECOND SEASON

The year 1967 was pivotal in politics and culture alike. The dawning of the age of aquarius had arrived as of January 14, when thousands of acid-inspired flower children gathered at the San Francisco Human Be-In. In was an auspicious start to a year that would challenge the rock-hard mores of conservative America. The war in Vietnam had cast a pall over a divided nation. The rise of student militancy and the Black Panthers upped the ante of anti-establishment. Protests and riots were now almost daily occurrences on the campuses and in the ghettos of urban America.

Meanwhile, in Haight-Ashbury and selected pockets across the universe, a whole new society — the drug culture — was arising. Teenyboppers had grown into teeny-poppers of LSD. Hippies were now the dandied punks of a disenfranchised generation whose operative words were peace and love. Psychedelia, best epitomized by the Jefferson Airplane, was all the rage. The Monterey Pop Festival had ushered in a newly-defined era of rock 'n' roll where aesthetics replaced the old bump 'n' grind. The Beatles, as usual, led the way with "Sgt. Peppers," an album simulating the ecstasy of an acid trip. Not far behind were the dark, brooding bands inspired by the lyricism of Bob Dylan — the Doors, the Velvet Underground and the Jimi Hendrix Experience. All in all, it was a banner year in rock history.

The Monkees, older and wiser. "The four young Monkees weren't fooled for a moment," wrote Timothy Leary. "They went along with the system but they didn't buy it."

Swept up in this tide of change were the biggest, best-selling band of the year: the Monkees. In one short year, they, and an entire youth generation, had evolved from innocent ersatz Beatlemania to jaded hippie anarchy. Shedding the silly mod uniforms of yore, the Monkees let their freak flags fly. There would be no more bubblegum for these boys.

But would the enlightened masses accept a Monkees metamorphosis or would the group forever be caught in the Catch-22? This question had not eluded the wary members of the Monkees. "I used to be a hippie. Tell me about a group like the Monkees and I'd sneer," Nesmith admitted to *Seventeen*. "I'm not that way anymore."

It was the Monkees' fervent hope that their new album, "Headquarters," would forever silence their critics. Never before or after would the group rally around a single project like they would "Headquarters." "It was a labor of love for all those guys," recalls Chip Douglas, who produced the album under his real name, Douglas Farthing Hatlelid. "They really wanted an album of their own."

The ardous process of generating an entire album's worth of original music took six weeks of anxiety and toil. By far the most inhibiting factor was the group's experience, or lack thereof, in the recording studio. According to Douglas, "they could hardly play. Mike could play adequate rhythm guitar, Peter could play piano but he'd make mistakes, and Micky's time on the drums was erratic, he'd speed up or slow down. That was the hardest part of it all — Micky beginning the drums... he would try hard, at least he would play all the way through a take. Peter had a tendency to stop in the middle of a take after he made a mistake. He'd say, 'hey, Micky, you're not doing the right thing on the drums.' I kept wanting to say to those guys, 'look, don't stop. Let me stop it if something goes wrong, you guys keep going.' "

Tensions quickly began to surface, further complicating an already formidable task. Each member had their individual ego at stake, as Tork reported in *When The Music Mattered*: "Davy played nothing but tambourine... so he had his part down after the second take, and we would sometimes do fifty takes to get our basic track down. Davy's arm got tired. He got sick of banging the tambourine all day long. And Micky lost faith in himself. He never did believe he was a decent drummer, so he didn't want to do it anymore. Mike wanted to produce his own records. He wanted to have total control. I was the only one who believed in the group per se, and so there I was all by myself, wanting a group, with nobody to be a group with."

Jones bears out Tork's evaluation of the situation. "It took us six valuable weeks to do it," says Jones of "Headquarters." "You know at the time we were all sitting around, knocking ourselves, saying, 'well, man, we don't play our own music,' so we went in and made 'Headquarters' and, God, it was grinding."

This rare shot from the ''Headquarters'' session was later replaced on the back cover. Chip Douglas (standing) and Hank Cicalo (seated) joined the heads. (Photo reproduction by Linda S. Johnson)

After the stinging attacks of the media, the Monkees took pains to make "Headquarters" as authentic as possible. No outside studio whizzes were allowed to interfere with the proceedings, except on the song "Shades of Gray," which featured a cello and a French Horn. Even Douglas, an expert bass player, was relegated to the second string, although, thankfully, he did manage to slip into the mix. The management was literally bending over backwards to insure the Monkees' artistic aspirations were met. Douglas remembers, "the hierarchy, Bert and Bob, kept advising me not to play with the group. They wanted the guys to have their chance."

Like so many crucial Raybert decisions, this policy was probably ill-advised. In the final analysis, a middle course between the Monkees and outside studio players (as on their next LP "Pisces, Aquarius, Capricorn and Jones, Ltd.") would prove to be the perfect balance. And, yet, the endearing amateurism and heartfelt intentions of "Headquarters" make it one of the more fascinating rock documents of its day. In perhaps no other era of pop music could a manufactured band demand and win the chance to record their very own album. In this way, "Headquarters" was truly a first.

Although the results were mixed, the Monkees' third LP remains one of the band's (they could now be called a band) top achievements. Without overreaching their grasp, the boys assembled a modest slew of pleasant songs, which they bang out with typical garage-band spirit. The decision to leave in the frequent slips, goofs and guffaws lent a certain self-effacing humor to the whole affair, best epitomized by "Band 6," (i.e. "Micky practices the drums") and the false starts of the lead-off track, Nesmith's "You Told Me." Another novelty track, in the tradition of "Gonna Buy Me A Dog" and "Your Auntie Grizelda," is "Zilch," a classic bit of psychobabble concerning a Mr. Bob Dobolina.

Beyond all the high jinks of "Headquarters" were several stand-out musical moments. Mann and Weil's "Shades Of Gray," a lilting ode to times past, featured choice vocals by both Jones and Tork. In fact, the song remains one of Tork's finest efforts on vocals, something that was hardly his strong suit. "I compare him vocally to Ringo Starr," says Douglas of Tork's pipes. "He had questionable pitch." Another Tork highlight, his co-written "For Pete's Sake," would later surface as the closing theme during the TV series' second season. Nesmith delivers another strong original, "You Just May Be The One," while injecting an overall country twang to the album. As usual, however, Dolenz steals the show. On the Little Richard-style rocker, "No Time," Dolenz foreshadows his growing affinity for soul music. But the highlight of "Headquarters" is the final track, Dolenz's "Randy Scouse Git," a wild, vamping protest number, complete with scat singing, which Micky pulls off with loose-limbed aplomb.

Surprisingly, the critics rose to the Monkees defense in their regard for "Headquarters." *Melody Maker's* review, in particular, lent new credence to the brand name Monkees. "The Monkees are in a strange position. They came into pop backwards with a huge reputation custom-built for them," wrote *Melody Maker*. "It's a tribute to Dolenz, Tork, Nesmith and Jones that the Monkees are equalling the high standards of their competitors and are even moving ahead of them."

Within the group's ranks, opinions seem divergent regarding the quality of "Headquarters." "The recording techniques are really, really more advanced now," Jones contends. "You can hear how thin it is and how puny we all sound."

Tork, who later admitted that some of his happiest moments as a Monkee were during the recording of "Headquarters," counters, "I think that album is a very young band with a lot of enthusiasm and promise and as such the album stands up today. It's not a mature rock band by any stretch but I think the music shows a lot of inventiveness and energy. I think it's a very good album for its time and place."

Unfortunately for the Monkees, the time and place could not have been worse. Only one week after the release of "Headquarters," the entire music community would turn its ear to the Beatles' "Sgt. Pepper's Lonely Hearts Club Band," which promptly bumped the Monkees' new LP off the top spot on the charts. For several months, the two albums would vie for top honors, with "Headquarters" invariably one notch lower than the Beatles' vaunted masterpiece. As Douglas readily admits, " 'Headquarters' seemed like amateur hour by comparison. It lacked heavy rock tracks." Another thing it lacked was a single, although it managed to move three million copies anyway.

Obscured by the vast shadow by "Sgt. Peppers," the Monkees' efforts to win over older fans and, thus, respectability had been in vain. Their hard-fought struggle to cut the strings of their image as puppets had all been for nought. "They were determined to overcome that image," Douglas confers. "But even when 'Headquarters' came out, people were still asking me, 'is it true those guys don't play their own instruments?' " Apparently, the ghost of "The Man With The Golden Ear" was destined to haunt the Monkees to their dying days as a band.

Still, the group carried on bravely and proudly in the face of reality. Having "proved" themselves on vinyl, the four Monkees set out to conquer their rabid faithful with a slam-bang live show. This time, Bobby Hart's Candy Store Prophets would stay behind in tinsel town. Instead, the Monkees would go at it alone, confident of their capabilities. "In terms of putting on a show," Nesmith told Rhino Records, "there was never any question in my mind, as far as the rock 'n' roll era is concerned, that we put on probably the finest rock 'n' roll stage show ever. It was beautifully lit, beautifully costumed, beautifully produced. I mean, for Chrissakes, it was practically a revue."

The choreography of the show remained similar to the previous tour. After bursting onstage through mock Vox speakers and running through a quick rendition of their biggest hits, the individual band members took turns in the spotlight. Although the program often varied, the basic musical styles of the solo set remained the same: Tork played a folk tune on the banjo, Dolenz ran through his elaborate James Brown "capes routine," and Jones sang an Anthony Newley number, such as "Gonna Build Me A Mountain" with considerable histrionic effect. Throughout the solo spots, the members were backed by the opening act, the Sundowners.

A rapid pace was maintained throughout the one-hour set via costume changes and Monkee-brand clowning. The climax of the show was usually a sing-along "Steppin' Stone" followed by a psychedelic rave-up complete with feedback, strobe lights and Dolenz flailing away at the tympany

(Photo by Henry Diltz)

(Photo by Henry Diltz)

The Monkees live in concert. After bursting through mock Vox speakers, the four idols put on a dazzling show, including an early psychedelic light display. Like the Beatles, they could barely hear themselves play. (Photos by Henry Diltz)

drums. Hence, the Monkees became one of the first major bands to experiment with the psychedelic light shows that were to become an obligatory part of every rock concert. So new were these pyrotechnics at the time that many of the in-concert light operators initially balked at the mere suggestion of waving a spotlight randomly. "Tours weren't quite as sophisticated back then as they are now," explains Bobby Dick, bassist of the back-up Sundowners. "A lot of reasons why is that you had these old-timers in the lighting department because of their union cards — they'd been union lighting men for thirty years. So if they were good enough for Lawrence Welk, they were good enough for the Monkees. So you had a lack of communication. They didn't like us because we were long-haired screwballs. It was the blue collar ethic against the faggot musicians."

Unfortunately, the import of the Monkees' concert innovations was often lost on the screaming pre-teens in attendance. "It wouldn't have mattered what we were playing and it seldom did," Dolenz told Rhino Records. "You couldn't hear a thing. No matter what we said, what we did, what we played, we could have just as soon had all the instruments turned off. Which is too bad, because after all the criticism, we really worked hard for weeks and weeks."

Nesmith, too, found little satisfaction in the live concert experience: "There was a feeling of consistently being on the brink. Of what I don't know. It's that strange anticipatory feeling that you go through before you get laid, before you have a great meal, before you get in a fight. It's an incredible anticipatory feeling that continues, but it's never satisfied. . . . The concerts were not orgasmic for me."

Despite their artistic reservations, the Monkees soon undertook their most extensive tour as a group. Under the aegis of the evergreen Dick "Rate-A-Record" Clark, the tour would touch down in every major market, including the showcase cities of New York and Los Angeles. First stop, in fact, was right in the Monkees' own backyard at the prestigous Hollywood Bowl. Unlike the previous tour, which opened timidly in Hawaii, this time the boys would play smack dab in the eye of the hurricane for all the skeptics to see.

On June 9, the toast of the town turned up to pass judgement on pop's latest prodigies. With Ike and Tina Turner as their opening act, the Monkees would have to be razor sharp in order to cut the mustard. As usual, the group rose to the occasion. The only hitch occurred at the end of the show when Dolenz committed the ultimate no-no at the Bowl — at a strategic moment in the set, with all eyes cast upon him, he astounded the patrons by acrobatically somersaulting into one of the fountains adjacent to the stage. Needless to say, the Monkees were never invited back to the Hollywood Bowl. Overall, however, the show was a triumph, proving once and for all that the Monkees could swing with the best.

One week later, Dolenz and Tork ventured up the coast to the Monterey Pop Festival. What they witnessed would change them, and the music industry profoundly. Among the acts who performed at the three-day festival were the Who, the Mamas and the Papas, Simon and Garfunkle, and Ravi Shankar. The San Francisco sound, á la the Airplane and the Dead, also made its mark. Three performers, however, stole the show — Otis Redding, Janis Joplin and an unknown fellow named Jimi Hendrix. Up until this time, Hendrix had been a prophet without honor in the States. To gain recognition, he sailed overseas to England, where he quickly established a reputation with his British backing band, the Experience. Dolenz, who had caught Hendrix's pyrotechnic stage act in London, now watched intently as Jimi wooed the acid-addled "love crowd" with walls of feedback. By the time Hendrix did his guitar-burning encore of "Wild Thing," Dolenz knew he had found a backing act for the Monkees' impending tour that even the most jaded of critics could not ignore.

Before the Monkees' summer tour could officially get under way, however, the group took a brief sojourn across the Atlantic. First stop was Paris, where Rafelson filmed the Monkees cavorting madly around famous Parisian landmarks for a future episode entitled "The Monkees in Paris," which aired late in the second season. Next stop was London, where Monkeemania was spiralling to staggering new peaks. With Dolenz's "Randy Scouse Git" (released as a single in England under "Alternative Title") topping the charts, the band would make their first and only concert appearances in the U.K. Promoted by none other than Brian Epstein, the Wembley Pool shows were the event of the season with London's rock aristocracy, such as the Clown Prince himself, Keith Moon, in attendance.

The Monkees, as usual, did not fail to please. Nor did they avoid controversy — both Nesmith and Dolenz sported black arm bands in a show of solidarity for Mick Jagger and Keith Richards, who had been jailed in a recent drug bust. With Lulu as their support act, the Monkees put on a show that had critics raving. *Melody Maker* was particularly impressed by the smash-up climax of the performance. "With noise and screams," the reviewer wrote, "I suddenly realized the Monkees were actually freaking out properly, and much better than many of the much vaunted psychedelic groups."

Dolenz in a purple haze at the Monterey Pop Festival. David Crosby (right) looks on. (Photo by Jim Marshall)

Back in the States, the Monkees launched their two-month American tour in Jacksonville, Florida. Instead of trekking like most bands in a tour bus, the Monkees travelled in style on their own airplane (complete with the Monkees' guitar logo), which jetted them to and fro in first-class comfort. Coming along for the ride were the opening acts, the Sundowners, the Jimi Hendrix Experience and Australian singer Lynne Randell. Teen-zines quickly picked up on the amorous intentions between Jones and Randell by splashing their glossy pages with ample photos of the two love birds at play.

The general atmosphere surrounding the tour was that of a party out of bounds. Police escorts met the group in every city in order to protect them from potential airport riots. The airplane, a huge four-engine turbo prop, became the Monkees' playpen in between gigs. The entire entourage would sneak to the back of the plane, where they would pass spliffs and sip champagne laced with Jimi's white lightning. No extravagance was spared for the Monkees or their fellow travellers. "One of the nice things about the Monkees," remembers Bobby Dick, "is that they were true to their old friends. You don't always get that kind of camaraderie once someone makes it — that helping hand doesn't always come down from the top. It was nice to see that friendship made a difference."

Controversy, however, was waiting in the wings. Clearly, the billing of the Monkees and Hendrix was doomed from the very start. Not only were the musical styles poles apart, so were the audiences. It was strictly soda pop versus psilocybin in terms of the musical mix. Why Hendrix ever agreed to go along with this plan is perhaps the greatest mystery of all. Several months prior to the tour, *Melody Maker* had asked for his opinion on the Monkees. Hendrix's response: "Oh God, I hate them! Dishwater. I really hate somebody like that to make it so big. You can't knock anybody for making it, but people like the Monkees?"

Obviously, the spectre of big bucks and publicity had changed Jimi's tune — either that or "Headquarters" had magically inspired a religious conversion to Monkee music. Either way, the cacophonic strains of Hendrix's feedback orgies mixed with his lascivious sexuality was clearly too much for the innocent bopper girls in attendance. "It was difficult for Jimi," Dolenz says, "because the kids were there to see us primarily. He didn't have much recognition at the time, so it was very strained as far as he was concerned. We had much more fun offstage than on, at the hotels and in the airplane."

One such offstage incident was reported in hilarious detail by Tork in *Crosby, Stills and Nash:* "We were in this hotel room. Jimi and Stephen (Stills) were sitting on these beds facing each other, just flailing away on acoustic guitars. In between 'em was Micky Dolenz, slapping his guitar like,

Soda pop versus psylocybin: Jimi Hendrix on tour with the Monkees.
Only a few months before, Jimi declared, "Oh God, I hate them!
Dishwater!" (Photo by Nona Hatay)

'slap, whacka, slap, whacka, slap.' And all of a sudden Micky quit. Then Stephen and Jimi stopped and Stephen said to Micky, 'Why'd you stop playing?' Micky said, 'I didn't know you were listening.' So there's one for ya — Hendrix, Stills, and Dolenz."

The fun was short-lived, however. After a handful of gigs, Hendrix grew sick of the "We want the Monkees" chant that met his every performance. Finally, he flipped the bird at the less-than-enthusiastic crowd at Forest Hills Stadium in New York and stormed offstage. With no malice towards the Monkees, he quit the tour to go solo. In order to cover up the circumstances behind his departure, a publicity release was circulated, claiming the Daughters of the American Revolution had found Hendrix's stage act too erotic.

It was a classic put-on, a tongue-in-cheek joke for those in the know. Not surprisingly, this thinly-guised ruse managed to go down — like so many Monkees inaccuracies — as historical fact in many rock chronicles. The DAR story was, of course, completely fabricated or, in the words of Dolenz, "a load of rubbish. He got a hit record off the tour, it must have been 'Purple Haze.' Obviously his audience was going to be quite different from ours and so we released him from the tour in New York so he could headline on his own."

The Hendrix travesty caused little or no harm to the Monkees, who were, by now, almost beyond criticism, having had so much negative publicity precede them. Anyway, the band was on a roll. Every stop of the summer tour was a financial and critical triumph. SRO crowds affirmed that Monkeemania was no flash-in-the-pan phenomenon. The band even turned down a lucrative opportunity to duplicate the Beatles' highly-publicized Shea Stadium appearance. Their policy was to never subject their fans to the impersonal stadium gigs that many of the mega-groups at the time accepted.

Every business move was now scrutinized by the Monkees for its creative significance. No longer would their artistic sensibilities be compromised by the holy buck. Nowhere was this attitude more prevalent than on their latest release, "Pleasant Valley Sunday"/"Words," which quickly became the band's fourth consecutive million-selling single, peaking at number three behind the Beatles' "All You Need Is Love" and the Doors' "Light My Fire." Written by the ever-tasteful tunesmiths, Gerry Goffin and Carole King, "Pleasant Valley Sunday" was the group's first blatant stab at relevancy (save for Dolenz's "Randy Scouse Git"). As such, it has been criticized over the years for its somewhat banal attack on suburban values — hardly a revolutionary topic of the times. Looking past the heavy-handed message, however, the song was a telling by-product of the Monkees' newfound artistic license. Benefitting from a crisp Douglas production, "Pleasant Valley Sunday" showcases the Monkees' sense of ensemble, from Dolenz's soaring vocals and Tork's skillful keyboards to Nesmith's catchy riffing. The B-side, Boyce and Hart's "Words" is less successful, but at least it showed no traces of Kirshner-inspired bubblegum.

By the end of the summer tour, the Monkees were at their confident peak as a performing unit. They were now in the exalted ranks of rock's ephemeral royalty and if anyone doubted it all they had to do was to check out the *Billboard* album charts on August 26:

1. Sgt. Peppers — The Beatles
2. Headquarters — The Monkees
3. Flowers — The Rolling Stones
4. The Doors — The Doors
5. Surrealistic Pillow — The Jefferson Airplane

Every angle of popular culture had been cornered by the Monkees — television, radio, records, concerts and magazines. Even pristine Ann Landers, the bellwether of Yankee Doodle mores, carried the news:

> Dear Ann Landers: I am a fourteen-year-old girl who spent six dollars to hear the Monkees give a concert last night. It was one of the greatest experiences of my life. Something happened at the hall and I need to know if I was right or wrong. My girlfriend and I were screaming a lot which is only natural when the Monkees perform. A middle-aged woman about thirty was sitting in front of us. After the second number she turned around and said, "If you kids don't stop screaming in my ear I am going to scream in yours."
>
> — Monkee Lover

> Dear Lover: If you screamed in church or at the ballet, I would say the woman had a right to complain. But screaming at a Monkees concert is not only in order, it is practically compulsory.

Now that the critics had begun to ease up on them, the Monkees began to address a comparison that had dogged them from their early days: the Beatles. At first, the Monkees had bowed deferentially towards their predecessors. They not only bowed, they scraped: "They're the greatest. What can I tell you?" Jones told the *New York Times*. "If we can only be one-quarter as good... or maybe a tenth?"

One dizzy year later, Jones had changed his tune. "We're not the Beatles yet — we're not that good — but there's as much difference between our first two albums and our new one, 'Headquarters,' as between the Beatles' first album and their sixth, 'Rubber Soul,' " Jones claimed to *Seventeen.*

Nesmith did not demur to the fab four as had Jones. He told *Seventeen*, "In a way we're bigger than the Beatles ever were. They had long hair, they were a little odd, but apart from their music, they didn't stand for anything. Even their music didn't have any message. But we stand for something — freedom! The Beatles are the Beatles, but the Monkees are Peter, Micky, Mike and Davy, four individuals."

If success had swelled the Monkees' heads, then it was up to Raybert to cool them down. "I remember times when the Monkees came in and said, 'we're bigger and better than the Beatles,' " Rafelson recalls. "I had to sit them down and say, 'now look, for Godsakes, don't get caught in this trap. You have a television show on the air every week and it's immensely popular but it's really the force behind your records.' "

Oddly enough, the Beatles actually did respect their illegitimate cousins, the Monkees. Lennon reportedly once remarked to Nesmith, "I think you're the greatest comic talents in film since the Marx Brothers. I've never missed one of your programs." Further proof of mutual respect between the two groups was the friendships that developed amongst the members. Interestingly, each Monkee befriended a different Beatle — Dolenz hung out with McCartney, Jones hit it off with Ringo and Tork found spiritual kinship with Harrison and later appeared in his "Wonderwall" film (not the album, as commonly reported).

Not surprisingly, the brooding artistic temperaments of Nesmith and Lennon also meshed. Nesmith later told *GQ*, "I'd spent four or five days with him in London when he was doing 'Sgt. Peppers' and there was an odd camaraderie between us. He really understood that ours was a television show, that we weren't a group. But we were caught up in the same sort of foment. In his case it was serious respect. In my case it was just media hype, yet there wasn't any difference."

If any doubts lingered in the hearts of Beatle/Monkee fans, *Melody Maker* dispelled them in a poll designed to determine which group was more popular. Of 99 people polled, 61 favored the Beatles over the Monkees. What had been proven? "John Paul, George and Ringo," the magazine concluded, "you're still in command."

Eight miles high the boys would sneak to the back of the plane and turn on "Sgt. Pepper". Notice the security guard. (Photo by Henry Diltz)

Ironically, the same schisms that wrenched apart the Beatles were wearing away at the Monkees. Like the Beatles, each Monkee had a particular appeal and a corresponding following. Jones was the teen heartthrob among the bunch; Nesmith appealed to the intellectual nebbish crowd; Dolenz won fans with his free-wheeling, wise-cracking demeanor. Tork's appeal, much like Harrison's, was more difficult to pinpoint. His empty-headed caricature on the television series contrasted the gentle "peace, love and flowers" image he developed off-screen. Still, he was a looker.

The foursome that jelled collectively on record, stage and screen never really grew close together offstage, however. There were two extremes — Dolenz and Jones struck up a lasting friendship; Nesmith and Tork barely tolerated each other. As far as the other intra-relationships were concerned, they were masked in public fraternity, although, in private, they were bearable at best. Dolenz told Rhino Records, "we were just crazy at this time because of the popularity and our egos and because we weren't a rock 'n' roll group before. In rock groups that have been together for years and years, the guys are usually pretty much alike, that's why they get along. Well, we were four of the most different people in the world. It was hard to get us together to do a show, much less a press picture."

The glue that kept the project from self-destruction was the open-door policies of Rafelson and Schneider, who encouraged the group to voice their grievances. "Our offices were a place to come and cooperatively air ourselves and work together," says Rafelson. "That was largely due to Bert Schneider. He just felt it was better to do it that way and God knows we spent hours doing it. Sometimes it was just a lot of babble but because people were given respect as opposed to saying, 'contractually you're full of shit, get out of here,' it was harmonious."

Although the group never really hit it off among themselves, Dolenz maintains "eventually we got close, much closer on the television show than in music, because there was such a polarity in the music — especially Peter and Mike. We were very competitive with each other, but it was a healthy competition, like coming up with the funniest lines."

By the start of the second season of filming, the Monkees were already seasoned pros in front of the cameras. As a result, things were a good deal looser on the set. Instead of five days, episodes were now routinely wrapped up in 2 1/2 days. The format of the show also loosened — inside jokes, political swipes and sly parodies of other TV shows snuck into the final edit with greater frequency than before.

In order to appease the temperaments of their headstrong stars, Rafelson and Schneider permitted the group greater creative license over the show. Both Dolenz and Tork took advantage of this freedom by directing an installment of the series. Dolenz's episode, entitled "Mijacgeo" (an amalgam of the names of Dolenz's family, Michael, Janelle, Coco and his late father George) was a surrealistic tour-de-force, co-written by Dolenz with Jon Anderson. Also known as "The Frodis Caper," this episode was the final installment of the series and the only one not produced by Raybert (Ward Sylvester produced).

Another concession to the four Monkees were the hand-picked guest stars that each of the boys chose to appear in the penultimate episodes. Among these guest celebrities were Tim Buckley, Frank Zappa and Charlie Smalls, who later wrote the musical "The Wiz." These calculated moves by Raybert helped to temper any dissension that might develop within the ranks. Each Monkee was now allowed to express their individual artistic desires without fear of corporate recrimination. This new autonomy had a profound impact on the television series, whose helter-skelter approach grew less linear and more disjointed as a result. Signs of this change were everywhere — from Dolenz's unkempt afro to the group's paisley gear. Canned laughter, the staple of all sitcoms, was scrapped altogether.

More than ever, the show exuded the spontaneous charm that was its trademark. "We improvised almost the entire show," Dolenz claimed to Rhino Records. "Many people think we were all puppets with strings attached to our mouths, and in many political and business ways we were. But as far as the television show went all the dialogue and the improvisation was almost all us. A good eighty per cent."

Like every group of the era, the Monkees embraced the Summer of Love with beatific resolve. Their image and their music showed signs of maturity. (Photo by Henry Diltz)

The second season: make room for Dada. Scripts? Who needs scripts? (Photo by Henry Diltz)

Nesmith, however, disagrees, saying, "On one hand it was a very carefully scripted and put-together show. On the other hand, the scripts provided a launching platform for the way we actually did it, which included some ad-libbing. But we didn't make up the situations, we always went back to the scripts."

Improvised or not, the general atmosphere on the set was quite convivial the second time around. A goof-off room, adjacent to the set, was built so the boys could practice music and expand their consciousness. "It was wonderful," recollects Tork. "They built a great big refrigerated room where we could set up amps and play guitars without the sound creeping back into the soundstage." Although hardly a den of iniquity, the room became a smoking parlor of sorts. "Typical of that confusion, we would have alfalfa sprout lunches and vegetarian burgers and then smoke grass," says Tork.

Drugs made their impact in varying degrees. Like every rock group at the time, the Monkees dabbled in psychedelics. The effects of their chemical adventures were felt to a greater extent in their music than on television, although Tork later told *Goldmine,* "There was one very real acid trip I took and they had to shoot around me. We had this Hawaiian thing and we were supposed to be wearing skirts and I just said, 'that's too much.' So I shined on them for a day." Nesmith, it turns out, shined on three complete episodes in the second season, not out of drug usage, but over artistic differences.

Still, nosy reporters tried to pry lurid tales of drug orgies from the Monkees every chance they got. *Melody Maker* reported one such incident at a British press conference: "A reporter with a quite unusual talent for picking the obvious, asked their opinion on drugs. The four Monkees fell about with laughter. 'That's the one we were waiting for,' yelled Micky.

" 'I took aspirin once,' said Peter as the general hilarity subsided. 'It disturbed my head and provided me with all my inspiration.'

" 'I take Exlax,' said Davy. 'it keeps me going all the time.' "

The full effects of drug experimentation were crystallized in the Monkees' fourth album, the excellent "Pisces, Aquarius, Capricorn and Jones, Ltd." Track for track, "Pisces, Aquarius" is arguably the finest album ever produced by the Monkees. Surprisingly, it was almost indiscriminately patched together between shoots. "This last album was completed in nine days," Nesmith told *Hit Parader* about "Pisces, Aquarius." "It's been cut in our own time between TV rehearsals and everything else. How creative can you be in that amount of time?"

The answer, of course, was in the grooves. Released in November, 1967, "Pisces, Aquarius" was the only Monkees album that managed to achieve a cohesive sound throughout. The reasons for this success seem varied. Without a doubt, drugs had an influence, particularly on the psychodelic "Daily Nightly." A more important factor than chemical enlightenment in dictating the album's final outcome was the lack of studio time available for its preparation. Instead of personally toiling for six weeks as they had with "Headquarters," the Monkees were forced to employ the services of hand-picked studio professionals such as renowned banjo picker Douglas

As a unit they were never very close, but on "Pisces, Aquarius" the Texas twang of Nesmith, the purist folk of Tork, the vaudevillian camp of Jones, and the rock'n'soul of Dolenz finally jelled. (Photo by Henry Diltz)

Dillard. The result was a cleaner, more polished sound and overall, a more assured production by Chip Douglas.

Credit must also go to Nesmith, who cast a watchful eye and exercised creative control over the entire proceedings. In the past, Nesmith had merely clocked in with a few choice cuts and then split. Douglas recalls that Nesmith "mainly wanted to do his songs. If he could have done a whole album of his songs he would have been happy. He could be congenial and cooperative and get everybody playing on his two or three cuts and then he'd disappear."

On "Pisces, Aquarius," however, Nesmith's influence is felt from first track to last. It is with that unmistakable Nesmith twang that "Pisces, Aquarius" gets underway. The opening cut, "Salesman," establishes the cynical tone that pervades throughout. No longer, it seems, were the boys "too busy singing to put anybody down" as had been proclaimed in "The Monkees Theme." The next track, "She Hangs Out," a re-recorded version of Jeff Barry's banished B-side, is another sharp-witted selection. Perfectly suited to Jones' limited vocal abilities, this rocking version is far superior to the session previously held under Kirshner's supervision. One of the Monkees' most transcendent performances follows, Bil Martin's wistful "The Door Into Summer" (Although co-credited, Chip Douglas claims the song is entirely Martin's composition). Rounding out the first side is a Beatlesque triad of songs, "Love Is Only Sleeping," "Cuddly Toy" and "Words." Taken together, side one of "Piesces, Aquarius" is perhaps the most accomplished (and listenable) sides of any Monkee album.

Unfortunately, side two gets off to a slow start with the slightly sappy "Hard To Believe." The next track, however, is a Monkees' musical highlight, Michael Murphy's "What Am I Doing Hangin' Round?" Using the country-western idiom that so perfectly suited his vocal abilities, Nesmith really shines on this song. After the somewhat pointless nonsense of "Peter Percival Patterson's Pet Pig Porky" (yet another novelty cut), is the groundbreaking "Pleasant Valley Sunday." The next track, Nesmith's "Daily Nightly" is a naive and mostly unsuccessful stab at pyschedelia, although it is notable as one of the earliest appearances of a Moog synthesizer on wax. Using only the third Moog in existence (Buck Owens and Walter/Wendy Carlos apparently owned the others), Dolenz experimented with the able assistance of the late Paul Beaver on both "Daily Nightly" and the album's closing track "Star Collector." Written by Goffin and King, "Star Collector" is a rousing put-down of celebrity adulation, pre-dating the similar sentiments of the Stones' "Star Star" by several years.

If nothing else, "Pisces, Aquarius" proved once and for all that the Monkees possessed considerable musical talent. It remains one of the few albums that Monkeemaniacs can play for their cynical friends and foes without picking up the needle to skip embarrassing tracks. Even the cover art is tasteful and restrained. Ironically, the legacy of Kirshner is partially responsible for the success of "Pisces, Aquarius." Many of the stunning array of songwriters that contributed to the album were originally recruited by the Golden Ear, including Carole King, Gerry Goffin, Cynthia Weil, Barry Mann and Jeff Barry. Final credit must still go the Monkees, however, who not only brought in such talents as Michael Murphy and Harry Nilsson, but selected the material as well.

Although "Pisces, Aquarius" shot to the top of the charts, it was promptly bumped from number one by the Beatles (once again) and "Magical Mystery Tour." Still, the group had several reasons to celebrate. With each new release, they were scaling new peaks. Their latest single, "Daydream Believer," was to become their *fifth* consecutive million-seller and their third and last chart topper. Written by ex-Kingston Trio member John Stewart, "Daydream Believer" was an instant Monkees classic, featuring a superb arrangement by Shorty Rogers and a sterling Chip Douglas production. The B-side, which was recorded, like "Daydream Believer," during the "Pisces, Aquarius" sessions, was a jazzy number named "Goin' Down." One of the most daring and original of all Monkees productions, "Goin' Down" was also one of the few tracks written entirely by the band ("Zilch" and "Band 6," which do not technically qualify as songs, were also credited to all four Monkees). Although the song never appeared on a Monkees album, it remains one of their true hidden nuggets, particularly notable for Dolenz's stream-of-consciousness rapping and a brassy, big-band production (also credited for the first time to the Monkees alone).

Even more prestige was indirectly accorded to the group when the Nesmith-penned "Different Drum" became a smash hit by a group named the Stone Poneys, featuring an unknown vocalist named Linda Ronstadt. The single, which peaked at thirteen on the charts, turned many a skeptical head in the direction of Nesmith, who, for all his fussing and fighting, had yet to strike gold with any original Monkees compositions. Buoyed by this success, Nesmith would soon undertake a solo project with the help of Shorty Rogers named "The Wichita Train Whistle Sings" which would garner further acclaim.

If all this was not enough, *Billboard* awarded the Monkees the title of top group of 1967 in their year-end poll. The group also copped honors for top singles artists and for the top two albums, "More Of The Monkees" and "The Monkees." Overall, they had sold a whopping 35,000,000 records in one year, more than the Beatles and the Stones combined.

1967, an altogether triumphant year for the Monkees, would end on a silent sour note. That December, unbeknownst to Monkees fans, Jones married Linda Haines. Although the exact details of this secretive union are still shrouded in mystery, this deception needs little explanation — it was strictly a financial move. Even though the private lives of celebrities have often been deliberately tailored for public consumption, there was no excuse for perpetuating the myth of Jones' bachelorhood for almost two years (it was finally revealed in 1969). As time goes by, such an offense may seem minor, but for a group that struggled so hard and long to establish its integrity, it was an inexcusable move.

As it happened, 1967 would prove to be the final year of Monkeemania. The "Summer of Love" would soon be replaced by the year of revolt. By 1968, the bright optimism of the Great Society had been swept askance by the tremendous undertow of the Vietnam war. No one had much use for a bunch of frolicking Monkees amidst all the world's problems. In the span of one year, Richard Nixon would assume the presidency, Martin Luther King and Robert Kennedy would be assassinated and the original Monkees would be no more. By comparison, the demise of the Monkees would seem somewhat inconsequential.

The public, it seems, had lost its taste for pure pop, opting instead for the "heavy" sounds of the day. The foursome of Dolenz, Jones, Nesmith and Tork did not mourn the downward spiral of their popularity — they were more than satiated. "They were tired of being bubblegum. They weren't bubblegum types as individuals," Rafelson contends. "Now that the word had gotten out that the Monkees were not responsible for their own music, the older kids said, 'fuck the Monkees, let my kid sister watch them. I want to listen to Jim Morrison and Jimi Hendrix, not ersatz Beatle records.' And I think they took that to task."

At this point, the Monkees had other things on their minds. Slowly, the group was coming to grips with the Frankenstein that had been created in their image. Instead of viewing the project as a cohesive whole, each member now sought to get the most out of it for their separate designs. Nesmith took advantage of the recording studio, Dolenz furthered his directing career, while Jones clung to his teen-idol status and opened boutiques. Tork merely bided time until his contract expired. Quite obviously, they needed something dramatic to draw them together as a group. That thing was "Head."

Originally titled "Changes," the movie "Head" was the perfect vehicle to channel the Monkees' frustrations. Although it proved to be the apex of their artistic pursuits, "Head," like so many Monkees' projects, was borne out of bitter haggling and divisiveness. The four Monkees, wary of their past mistakes, made quite sure they had a stake in the creative process from the start. Rafelson recollects: "At this point, they had pretty swelled heads as the major pop stars of their time. They said, 'fuck it, we don't need a director, we'll write our own movie.' Jack came to me and said, 'these guys are mad — they think they're Marlon Brando!' "

The Jack that Rafelson refers to was none other than Jack Nicholson in his pre-superstar salad days. Trying to make his mark in Hollywood as a screenwriter, Nicholson had long labored in obscurity. An earlier Nicholson effort, "The Trip," which concerned the effects of an LSD experience on Peter Fonda, had been butchered by the censors. Nicholson had also tried his hand at acting, although mostly in such B-grade Roger Corman quickies as the legendary "Little Shop Of Horrors."

Rafelson, who was always an accurate judge of talent, saw great promise in Nicholson's varied abilities. Together, they conspired to write a wicked, dark parody of the entire Monkees phenomenon. The Monkees, however, would not permit such a project without their input, so the entire entourage (the four Monkees plus Rafelson and Nicholson) went off to the resort town of Ojai to write the movie together. "We all went down to someplace, Marina del Mar or something, for the weekend with a bag of Acapulco Gold," Jones later told the *Monkee Business Fanzine*, "and by the end we'd written the movie."

"They just wanted to feel like they were participating," explains Rafelson, "and I wanted them to participate." By the end of the weekend in Ojai, the sextet had devised the entire movie by extemporaneously talking into a tape recorder. Although each of the Monkees participated in this process, none were given screenwriting credit in the film. This inequity precipitated a brief stand-off between Raybert and the Monkees before the start of shooting. Nesmith, in fact, withheld the tapes recorded in Ojai until a settlement could be made.

The boys were no longer too busy singing to put anybody down. (Photo by Henry Diltz)

50

Chip Douglas (right) instructs Jones on vocals. "Daydream Believer" would be Douglas' last production and the group's final number one single. (Photo by Henry Diltz).

"When we first started filming the movie 'Head,'" Jones reports, "the only person they were filming was Peter because we didn't show up. We demanded to get paid prior to starting filming and they negotiated a horrendous $1000 for each of us as an advance to the movie and they were reluctant to give us that."

After the mini-strike was settled, the movie finally began its full-scale production. Still, it was not without its problems. Luckily, Nocholson saved the day. Tork recalls, "It was as much trouble making that movie as it was doing the TV show. For one thing, working for Rafelson is very difficult. He was not to me an artist's director. I was saved by the fact that Nicholson was on the set. I know there's one scene for sure I would never have gotten through if it hadn't been for Nicholson. And Nicholson, I think, is a master. The fact that Nicholson was involved in the project was the making of it."

Nesmith agrees, adding, "if you want to say who's vision the movie was, it was Jack Nicholson's. Jack is beyond world class, he's one of the greats. He's always had a remarkably creative, astute, impeccable sense of taste. What he brought to Ojai was what ultimately became the parameters of the movie."

Now that the Monkees were consumed in the production of "Head," they had little interest in returning to the recording studio. Colgems, on the other hand, desired new vinyl to followup on the chart success of "Daydream Believer." Without the Monkees' consent, they began scouring the vaults in search of some scraps to throw the awaiting public. The result was, artistically, the weakest single release to date, "Valleri"/"Tapioca Tundra." The A-side, to be fair, was a catchy, if somewhat pedestrian, Boyce and Hart tune that had been sitting in the cans for well over a year.

The evolution of the song, in fact, is an interesting story, more interesting perhaps than the song itself. Hart remembers, "Donnie kept telling us to write a girl's name song. So early one morning Tommy woke me up and said, 'I just told Donnie we wrote this great girl's name song and that we'd play it for him in a half-hour, so get up.' So I got up, took a shower, got in the car and on the way over there Tommy started playing some chords and shouting out as many girl's names as he could think of. Finally we came up with the name Valleri. So by the time we knocked on Donnie's door in Truesdale all we had was the word Valleri and a set of four chords. Donnie thought it was a smash."

Unfortunately for the eager tunesmiths, the Monkees were in the midst of their musical revolt and, thus, "Valleri" was relegated, for the time being, to the dusty shelves of Colgems. Kirshner did make sure, however, that the song snuck on to one of the episode's soundtracks, where it was recorded by two separate DJs in Chicago and Florida. After getting an avalanche of requests from listeners who had heard the bootleg version on the air, RCA decided to finally release "Valleri" on vinyl. Boyce and Hart went back into the studio and cut another version of the song, this time adding the fatuous horn arrangements that ultimately cluttered up the final released version (although sideman Louie Shelton's classical guitar licks were a nice touch).

The Monkees were far from happy to learn of Colgems' closed-door strategems. In fact, they were sufficiently incensed to demand that Boyce and Hart remove their names from the production credits. Nesmith also took liberal opportunities to slag the song, publicly declaring it the "worst song of all time" (alongside his other "worst of all time," "More Of The Monkees"). Despite the controversy, "Valleri" became the sixth and last million-selling Monkees smash, peaking at number three on the charts.

The loose-lipped Nesmith also had something to answer for: the B-side, "Tapioca Tundra." Stressing the weaker side of Nesmith's songwriting skills and vocals, this song was basically ill-conceived, saved only by some echoed vocal effects. Somehow the normally discerning Nesmith had lost the bouncy playfulness of his earlier efforts. Unfortunately, this tendency to lapse into senseless Tex-Mex babble would be fully realized on the next Monkees LP, "The Birds, The Bees and The Monkees." A mediocre record to begin with, "The Birds, The Bees and The Monkees" was practically sabotaged by Nesmith alone. Such half-baked offerings as "Magnolia Simms" and "Writing Wrongs" were so unlistenable they made Jones' thin originals seem like Gershwin by comparison. Even the trusty Mr. Dolenz commits the unpardonable sin of "Zor and Zam," which was little more than pseudo-Grace Slick ranting.

Dolenz with his bride-to-be Samantha Juste. The happy couple was pretty as a picture.
(Photo by Henry Diltz)

Overall, the less said "The Birds, The Bees and The Monkees" the better. Compared to its predecessor, "Pisces, Aquarius," "The Birds, The Bees and The Monkees" was nothing more than the two previous singles tacked together with a few outtakes. Although it is credited as the first full album production by the Monkees, Tork was strictly persona non grata with not a vocal or song to his credit. Overall, the album lacks the pop values and collective unity achieved during the reign of Chip Douglas. The Monkees had been musically manipulated once again, but unlike before, sales did not justify the mediocrity. In fact, it became the first album that failed to top the charts, though it did squeak briefly into the Top Five.

The follow-up single, "D.W. Washburn"/"It's Nice To Be With You" was another desperate attempt by the powers that be to milk the dying carcass for all it was worth. This time the group failed to crack the Top Ten, the first single not to do so. Two factors had contributed to this ignominious feat. First, the television show was now off the air and, secondly, a competing version by the Drifters may have weakened its appeal. Either way, it was rapidly becoming clear that Monkeemania was running dry.

The absence of new episodes, now that the second season had concluded, was truly the nail in the coffin. Without the weekly promotional push on the tube, the Monkees' records lacked the key ingredient of their success. An important question now lay in the balance — the bank balance, that is: would there be a third season of the show? Already, the series had been showing signs of

Backstage at a Monkees show, Jack Nicholson (with trademark eyebrows) pays his respects. Together, they would create "Head". (Photo by Henry Diltz)

atrophy, most visibly the self-effacing in-jokes that cropped up with greater frequency. "It was our way of saying to ourselves that we were running out of ideas," says director Frawley. "We knew we had squeezed it dry."

Rafelson and Schneider, sated by the Monkees success, were no longer interested in the grind of prime time — cinema was their new obsession. The Monkees themselves had no desire to carry on with the tried and true format of Davy meets girl, Monkees sing a song, Davy gets girl, Monkees sing another song. Instead, the four members submitted an entirely new format to NBC, who promptly rejected it. Then, in a joint resolution of the involved parties, the decision was made to cancel the series. An embittered Dolenz later explained the reasoning behind this self-termination. "We ended the show because the Establishment wanted it to go on exactly the way it was and we didn't," he fumed to *Melody Maker.* "The Establishment, of course, controls the money, but we knew that the series had to grow or die. They didn't want it to change, so we wouldn't do another series."

"We weren't greed freaks," Rafelson adds. "We had proved what we set out to prove. I think that when the TV show went off, a little of the bloom was off the plant — it didn't have that force." Another factor, no doubt, was the network competition, in particular, the long-running "Gunsmoke" which went head-to-head against "The Monkees" show during the second season. Nonetheless, the series did manage to, once again, garner two more Emmy nominations, although they did not win.

Meanwhile, as Monkeemania continued its rapid descent in the States, the four Monkees lit out for friendly foreign soil in the Far East. In September '68, they travelled to Japan and Australia for a series of live venues. Apparently, their tarnished image at home had not translated abroad, where mob scene after mob scene greeted their every appearance. Their foreign fans cared not a whit if Peter wore a scraggly beard or if the group as a whole seemed slightly jaded by the adulation. The tour was wildly successful from both a critical and financial standpoint. It was also a welcome respite from the malignant decay of L.A. As fate would have it, this was to be their last tour as the original four Monkees.

The year 1968 was now grinding to a halt, as were the Monkees. With the show off the air, the band could hardly buy publicity. Even when Nesmith was busted in Beverly Hills for sporting a shirt made out of the American flag, no one, beyond the fan-mags, bothered to report the news. New teen-idols like Bobby Sherman (who had appeared on a Monkees episode) began to replace the smiling, white-teethed visage of Jones on the trend-conscious fanzines.

The changing of the guard in American pop culture now meant the Monkees were disposable — they would soon be relegated to cut-out bins and attic drawers. So sick and tired were they of their flaccid phenomenon that the Monkees barely put up resistance to their imminent demise. "We were all very interested in our own individual egos and our own individual careers," reports Dolenz.

The irony, then, of belated industry respect was too much for the weary Monkees to bear. The hip rock journals, such as *Rolling Stone,* had now found it in their hearts to praise the ungrateful dead. "By definition, the Monkees are in another world," the magazine wrote in their expose on the L.A. scene, "but they are honest people, after all, and do fit in the scene quite well." It was a classic case of too little, too late, as far as the Monkees were concerned. They had no response for the newly-enlightened pundits who had so mercilessly flogged the group in the past. Their answer was on the movie screen — it was called "Head."

HEAD

A cinematic kiss-off to the monster they had created. "Head" was, in Nesmith's words, "the most bonafide example of the Monkees' collective thinking."

Unbeknownst to the Monkees and their creators, "Head" was destined to become their crowning glory as a creative unit — a cinematic kiss-off to the monster they had created. As such, it looms far and away above the ash-heap of rock movies that have attempted relevancy in the past. "It exposes much of what all rock groups went through but nobody had the guts to say," contends the film's co-writer and director, Bob Rafelson. "It's quite different than the Beatles' movies."

This is true. Whereas "A Hard Day's Night" sanitized the sexuality of the Beatles by portraying them as humorous and huggable lads, "Head" went straight for the jugular. In a series of surreal vignettes, the Monkees manage to puncture, deflate and ultimately reduce to shards their burdensome plastic image. The action — framed by a collective suicide attempt that opens and closes the film — is a quirky montage of visual puns, cutting satire and trippy music. Briefly entering the fray are such notable guest stars an Annette Funicello, Carol Doda, Teri Garr, Victor Mature, Sonny Liston and Frank Zappa. Throughout the wildly disjointed sequences, the only constant is the Monkees continual attempt to escape their public image. They have no control, however, over their destiny, which careens like a pinball from scene to scene.

From the murky waters of scholarly analysis, no one theory seems to sum up the philosophical import of this campy cult classic. Only one thing is agreed upon by the principals behind it all; that is, the overall worthiness of the project. The reasons, no doubt, for this harmonious viewpoint (perhaps the only such universally agreed upon topic in the history of the group) stem from the origins of the project in Ojai, where the movie was collectively written. " 'Head' was the most bonafide example of the Monkees' collective thinking," asserts Nesmith, who recalls the meeting of the minds in Ojai as "an intense, soul-searching weekend."

"When it came down to doing the feature we all took our clothes off, everybody got naked for that," says Rafelson. "It's the exposure of the whole myth — that's 'let's come out and tell the truth about this whole concept of having manufactured and manipulated them.' Let it be a movie that made their statement on the mess of it all."

"We were trying to make a film we'd appreciate without network censorship problems," contends "Head's" executive producer, Bert Schneider. From the very beginning, Schneider and Rafelson had wanted to move into film production. Now, here they were making a movie about the very project that had so dominated their lives in the past three years. Schneider was not without his misgivings.

Rafelson recollects, "Bert kept saying, 'look, for all you life you've talked about making a movie. For God's sake, why do you want to make the Monkees' movie?' And I said, 'because it's an incredible thing we've all been through, let's put it on film.' " If, however, both producers could have foreseen the resultant critical and financial "Head"-ache of their first movie producion, it likely would never have been attempted.

"The entire Monkees thing took place in a hostile environment," explains Nesmith. "Boy, I'll tell you, it was never more hostile than when 'Head' came out. Everyone was convinced at that point that it was some plot by the government to subvert the minds of youth."

Part of the problem stemmed from the disastrous promotional campaign mounted by the producers. "When we made 'Head,' Bob and Bert sweated their blood to make it a success," Tork later told *Blitz* magazine, "but they didn't sweat to push it the way they did our original television show. They got very esoteric." Instead of opting for the conventional newspaper flash, Rafelson and Schneider decided to explore the then-vogue theorems of Marshall McLuhan.

In his book, *Understanding Media*, McLuhan wrote that "ads seem to work on the very advanced principle that a small pellet or pattern in a noisy, redundant barrage of repetition will gradually assert itself." Taking his message on the medium to task, Rafelson and Schneider designed a subliminal, almost minimalist, ad campaign that featured only a close-up photo of a balding, slightly beatific man's head. Nothing but the word "Head" was even mentioned in the ad, not even that this was a movie starring the Monkees.

"The ad campaign," Tork argued "was not designed to get either the heads or the teenyboppers. The heads didn't want to see a Monkees movie, and the teenyboppers didn't want to see a head movie. So we got nobody. It's too bad. It's a movie that I know with the right promotion would have made a much bigger splash. It needed to be promoted over a long period of time... it wasn't instantly accessible."

Up against the wall, the Monkees face the critics. Despite negative reviews at the outset, "Head" has gone on to become a cult classic.

Rafelson explains: "At this time I thought the name Monkees was an anathema to the public. I was right. In fact, when the film opened the first night in the Village, people came storming out and demanded their money back because they found out the Monkees were in the picture." Indeed, the culture clash was inavoidable considering the prickly demographics of such a film. On the one hand, hip adult audiences would not be caught dead in a theatre running a movie by the beyond-contempt Monkees. On the other hand, by debunking and lampooning their prepubescent appeal, the film essentially devastated the very audience that had supported the group in the past.

"I certainly knew it wasn't going to be 'let's clamor for the Monkees' and bring in the seven-year-olds," asserts Rafelson, "because you don't have them starting off committing suicide in the movie if that's what you want to accomplish. The movie separates itself entirely from the television show."

The end result was a box-office thud of the first magnitude. After debuting at the Greenwich

COLUMBIA PICTURES Presents **the monkees**

"make an inventive, creative, first film!"
—*William Wolf, Cue Magazine*

"head"

"A movie for a turned-on audience!"
—*Renata Adler, New York Times*

G
Suggested for GENERAL audiences.

co-starring
Victor Mature! and **Sonny Liston!** and **Annette Funicello!** and **Carol Doda!**

Written and Produced by
BOB RAFELSON and JACK NICHOLSON • Executive Producer BERT SCHNEIDER • Directed by BOB RAFELSON

G TECHNICOLOR®

Hear The Monkees sing 'THE PORPOISE SONG' in the film and on the Colgems Soundtrack album.

and Cinema Studio Theatres in Manhattan, "Head" had an unceremoniously short run of three days and never did have a general release. The date of the debut, November 6, 1968, one day after Richard Nixon had narrowly defeated Hubert Humphrey in a bitterly contested presidential election, could not have been worse. In a darkly perverse way, "Head" had reflected the malignant cynicism of 1968. The brief snippets of war, including the summary execution of a Vietcong soldier, were generally misinterpreted by critics, who perceived them as smug and flippant commentary on the burning issue of the times.

Even the venerable first lady of film, Pauline Kael, misperceived the filmmaker's intent. Condemning the movie in a particularly savage attack in the *New Yorker*, Kael wrote, "the doubling up of greed and pretentions to depth is enough to make a pinhead walk out." Others interpreted incorrectly that "Head" was strictly a turn-on movie for dope fiends. The *New York Times* carried such a review, claiming it "might be a film to see if you have been smoking grass or if you like to scream at the Monkees, or if you are interested in what interests drifting heads and hysterical high-school girls."

As a result of such unforgiving and generally execrable critical attacks, the film sank without a trace, seemingly doomed to triple-bill grind houses and midnight movie cult status. Over the years, however, "Head" has steadily grown in stature. In France — the country that hails Jerry Lewis as a cinematic genius "Head" was overly-praised as a masterpiece of movie-making. Stateside, the film has also been accorded its due, with a respectable underground reputation to this very day.

One of the reasons behind this belated acclaim was the subsequent success of Rafelson and Schneider's highly respected BBS Productions. If "Head" had been held guilty by association with the Monkees, now it had been absolved by its association with BBS. The film is also notable as the first collaborative effort between Rafelson and Nicholson — an alliance that would later flourish in "Five Easy Pieces," "The King Of Marvin Gardens" and "The Postman Always Rings Twice."

After Rafelson's Oscar-nominated directorial splash with "Five Easy Pieces," "Head" was finally revived in a showcase setting at the Beverly Canon Theatre in 1973. This time, the film received its just desserts from a repentant critical community. Charles Champlin, the dean of critics at the *Los Angeles Times,* wrote of "Head": "Seen again, you wonder how the critics and the early audiences could have missed the film's fierce visual energy and perhaps even more the film's tart, iconoclastic point of view."

Some critics perceived the war scenes in "Head" as a smug and flippant commentary on the times.

Over the years, as other rock movies fade from raucous romps to staid period pieces, "Head" stands shoulders above its competition. "What's happening as time goes on is that the movie is becoming a chronicle of an age," reasons Tork. "At the time, it was just a chronicle of the Monkees."

More often than not these days, "Head" is interpreted as the Monkees' bittersweet swansong to pop culture. Nesmith, for one, begs to differ. "People always interpret it as the Monkees' swansong — suicide and good-bye. It's not so," he argues. "We were on a roll. We were at the top of our form, at the height of our popularity with a network television show, we were cooking. Now, with this motion picture deal, this would set us apart — it would make us a valid member of the community. We were going to boogie across the silver screen with a series of movies... who knew it would be a swansong? It wasn't designed that way."

There seems to be a general disagreement within the Monkees camp over Nesmith's assumption. Schneider, for instance, holds true to the widespread notion that "Head" was good riddance to the Monkees phenomenon. "We were quite satisfied to see the movie be the last thing the Monkees ever did," Schneider contends. "That was really what the goal was — that this was the cap and then we're finished and if we can destroy the group in the process of making the movie, all the better."

Quite possibly, the swansong theory developed out of the unremitting critical reception that met the film. To the Monkees, the resulting financial bust of "Head" all but shattered the already loose binds between the group. "It was unfortunate," says Nesmith of the film's failure. "It made me feel that this was a hole out of which there was no way to collectively climb. The environment was too hostile."

Even more unfortunate were the neglected musical efforts of the Monkees on the movie's soundtrack. The musical centerpiece of "Head" and the resulting soundtrack album was the stunning "Porpoise Song," a psychedelic nugget written by Gerry Goffin (who produced it) and Carole King. The brilliant aural sheen to "Porpoise Song" was provided by Jack Nitzsche, who arranged the song (and who also produced the vaguely reminiscent "Expecting To Fly," by the Buffalo Springfield). Other highlights included Toni Stern's lilting "As We Go Along," which was pre-released as the B-side of the "Porpoise Song" single. Several Monkees' originals were also worth noting. Tork contributed two solid efforts, "Can You Dig It?" and "Do I Have To Do This All Over Again?," while Nesmith kicked in the electric Bo-Diddley-rocker, "Circle Sky." Unfortunately, the superior live cut of "Circle Sky," recorded in concert for "Head," was replaced by the less explosive version on the subsequent soundtrack (the film version is available on the Australian "Monkeemania" compilation).

Strangely enough, the person behind the musical decisions was none other than Jack Nicholson, who presided as musical supervisor over the soundtrack. Although some have argued that Nicholson made a mess of the proceedings, the "Head" soundtrack has stood the test of time and remains, along with "Pisces, Aquarius," one of the few cohesive albums by the Monkees. Nicholson throws in snippets of dialogue and various sound effects to achieve a rich collage effect that is stylistically similar to the visual kitchen-sink construction of "Head." Due to the movie's instant obscurity, the soundtrack album has become one of the Monkees' true collectors items, with mint copies fetching upwards to forty dollars these days.

It is difficult to assess the lasting impact of "Head" in terms of cinematic influence. There is little doubt, however, that of all the Monkees endeavors "Head" will stand as the capstone of their careers. It remains a telling vindication of the still-persistent notion that the Monkees were nothing but bubblegum. All in all, "Head" is essential viewing for all Monkees aficionados and well worth seeking out for repeated viewings and further insights.

Undaunted by the castigation that met "Head," the Monkees launched immediately into a television special entitled, "33 1/3 Revolutions Per Monkee." It was to be their last project with the original line-up. The one-hour variety show was the first of three such Monkees' TV specials scheduled by NBC, although the other two never materialized. Nonetheless, "33 1/3" stands as one of the great lost artifacts of rock 'n' roll. Billed as a "psychedelic salute to the evolution of man and his music," "33 1/3" showcased, once and for all, the essence of the Monkees not as musicians, but as performers.

The special was the product of British director Jack Good, described by one writer as "the D.W. Griffith of pop style." Since the mid-'50s, Good had established a solid reputation within the British television industry for his innovative rock showcases, "6.5 Special," "Wham" and "Oh Boy." Inspired, no doubt, by the sardonicism of "Head," Good utilized the would-be test-tube origins of the Monkees to mock and deride the artful pretenses of the then-vogue conceptual rock bands.

"What made this film worthwhile," wrote George Melly of "33 1/3" in *Revolt Into Style*, "was that it demonstrated with a certain brilliance how yesterday's revolutionary can turn into today's reactionary. Good's enthusiasm is reserved for rock 'n' roll: sexy, extrovert, good dirty fun. When pop went highbrow it lost him. I dare say 'Sgt. Pepper' was his Waterloo, and he used this film to make this point with considerable panache. The Monkees were originally computerized into existence as plastic Beatles but have become, not only adequate performers, but discontented with their lot. Good used this discontent as the vortex of an inventive piece of nostalgia and attack."

The highlight of "33 1/3" is a rollicking non-stop ten-minute rock 'n' roll jamboree that features the star-studded talents of Jerry Lee Lewis, Fats Domino and Little Richard in a seamless medley of their greatest hits. Sandwiched in between these legendary rockers are the four Monkees, who, with greased-back hair and matching zoot suits, belt out ace renditions of "At The Hop" and "Little Darlin'." For pure rock 'n' roll ecstasy, this segment is perhaps the peak performance of the Monkees ever captured on celluloid.

Oddly enough, "33 1/3" is nearly dominated by the then-popular (but now obscure) Brian Auger and the Trinity with Julie Driscoll, a steely blues belter in the Annie Lennox tradition. Auger, who acts as the master of ceremonies, appears at the outset of the show, preaching demonically about the evolution of music. Finally he introduces the band: "Here they come, idolized, plasticized, psychoanalyzed and sterilized... the Monkees!" What follows is a captivating psychedelic destruction of the Monkees myth. Musical highlights include Dolenz's soul-fried rendition of "I'm A Believer," Nesmith's split-screen/personality "The Only Thing I Believe That's True" and a spectacular five-minute freak-out jam session that includes the Buddy Miles Express. The closing number, "Listen To The Band," stands as the last Monkees' performance with all four members on stage. As such, it is hard to think of a more apt swansong.

Unfortunately, "33 1/3" was buried by NBC, which scheduled the special head-to-head against the Academy Awards on April 14, 1969. Hence, the Monkees' last desperate gasp of creativity was, once again, snuffed. NBC was not taking any chances with this slightly off-kilter special — it seemed too subversive for John Q. Public. In fact, the real surprise is that "33 1/3" ever aired at all on network television. One can only imagine the poor ignorant souls that innocently flipped the dial during the Oscars only to tune into a most unorthodox program featuring robotic-dancing Monkees singing "I'm a wind-up man" with cogs and gears projected behind them. "33 1/3" was just not their speed.

Not that it really mattered to the Monkees. Immediately upon finishing "33 1/3," Tork gave notice — he wanted out of the group. Reportedly suffering from exhaustion, Tork was in dire need of a vacation. On December 30, 1968, he became a civilian again, but as later events would attest, he was hardly free of the Monkees.

The first act of the remaining threesome was to release a new LP, "Instant Replay." A better title might have been "Instant Relic." By now it was obvious that the group had lost all interest in their music. Of all the Monkees' original compositions on the album, only Jones manages some respectability with the excellent "You And I." Dolenz, who could always be counted on to contribute a sparkling gem or two, could now only manage the meandering drivel of "Shorty Blackwell." Boyce and Hart, buoyed by their success with "Valleri," resurfaced with several outtakes serving as warmed-over filler. The one bonafide highlight of the bubblegum jumble of "Instant Replay" is the polished Nesmith production of Goffin/King's lovely "I Won't Be The Same Without Her." In the end, Goffin and King were arguably the most consistently inspired of the

Four world-weary Monkees meet the press. "We got so fed up," Dolenz claimed, "that we didn't give a damn what people thought."

Monkees' songwriters. Among their impressive array of credits are "Take A Giant Step," "Pleasant Valley Sunday," "Star Collector" and "Porpoise Song."

Despite the doldrums of "Instant Replay" and the resultant lukewarm sales (it barely slipped into the Top 40), the threesome carried on in the face of plummeting fame. "A the time we got so fed up," Dolenz contends, "that we didn't give a damn what people thought." Just to prove the point, the band released a two-sided turkey as their next single — Boyce and Hart's "Clarksville" retread, "Tear Drop City," with Goffin/King's "A Man Without A Dream." Once again, the public virtually ignored the songs, which, for the Monkees, was probably just as well.

Considering their dismal returns, one would imagine that Screen Gems, in their infinite business wisdom, would lock the door and throw away the key on the remains of the Monkees. Publicity efforts were now being concentrated on Colgems stable-mates The Lewis and Clarke Expedition and Hoyt "Joy To The World" Axton. Even the flying nun herself, Sally Field, recorded a batch of songs for the growing label. Founding members, the Monkees, were now just one of many acts at Colgems. Nonetheless, Screen Gems signed the group to a extensive new contract which — finally — granted artistic license solely to the Monkees.

Under the guidance of their new managers, David Pearl and Brendan Cahill, the Monkees prepared to hit the road one last time. With several tours under their belts, the band was, by now, a professional ensemble onstage. An ambitious two-hour revue was choreographed, including wacky silent footage that was projected behind the band (shot by then-fledgling directors Nesmith and Dolenz). A backing band, Sam and the Goodtimers (formerly of Ike and Tina Turner) provided punchy R&B accompaniment as the Monkees knocked out their greatest-hits medley and an array of standards ranging from "Summertime" to "Johnny B. Goode." In place of the departed Tork were Bill Chadwick and John London, both long-time Nesmith buddies.

Unfortunately, attendance was marginal in comparison to the days of yore. The numbers kept dwindling as the band trekked bravely across the American heartland, playing to die-hard faithful. Several dates ended up being cancelled due to lack of ticket sales. Later, Dolenz candidly admitted that the tour "was like kicking a dead horse. The phenomenon had peaked."

After their final performance in Oakland, the disillusioned threesome spilled their guts to *Rolling Stone*. "Look," Dolenz told the interviewer, "the Monkees is the name of a TV show. I was hired to play the part of a rock and roll drummer, but what I am is an entertainer trying to reach an audience of eight-year-old girls. I'm no more a Monkee than Lorne Greene is a Cartwright."

One last ray of hope, the new single "Listen To The Band"/"Someday Man," renewed optimism within the ranks. The A-side, "Listen To The Band," was a country-flavored anthem marred only by the slightly self-aggrandizing applause at the end of the track. A solid Nesmith effort, it is also notable as the first A-side of a single release to be penned by a Monkee. The flip, Paul Williams' "Someday Man" is a breezy ballad that, for the first time, came from a non-Screen Gems copyright. On its own merits, the song made a slight dent on the charts, becoming Williams' first hit record.

Following close on the heels of "Listen To The Band" was the next single release "Good Clean Fun"/"Mommy and Daddy." This time both sides were Monkees' originals, which hardly mattered anyway, since the single barely eked into the Hot 100. The A-side, Nesmith's "Good Clean Fun" was a fairly pedestrian tune in the country mode. The B-side, Dolenz's "Mommy and Daddy" was far more interesting with its pointed lyrics á la "Randy Scouse Git."

The follow-up album, "The Monkees Present," was a slight improvement over "Instant Replay." Culling cuts from the previously released singles, the album also featured another fine selection from Michael Murphy, "Oklahoma Backroom Dancer." Judging from the meager sales, however, it was obvious that the end was near. The project had Peter-ed out, now it would Mike-out too. Having garnered critical accolades from his "The Wichita Train Whistle Sings" solo vehicle, Nesmith now turned his eye to forming The First National Band. First he had to settle the score with Screen Gems, a move which cost him well over $100,000 in unpaid wages from his recently-signed contract.

Nesmith gladly sacrificed the money. "You don't have to be blind to see a sinking ship," he told Rhino Records. "I think if the four of us had stayed together as time had turned around that maybe we could have ended up with another television show and perhaps done something meaningful. I didn't want to. I didn't enjoy working with the other fellows. And Screen Gems had exhausted their money-making machine. They weren't interested in whether or not we were good, understand, it was whether we could make any money for them."

With Nesmith gone, the two remaining Monkees — Dolenz and Jones—were practically non-entities as far as Screen Gems was concerned. To fulfill their contract, the duo were given a paltry $20,000 to go record an album ("It was a snow job," Jones sniffed years later). With Jeff Barry at the production controls, the two Monkees cranked out a perfunctory single "Oh My My"/"I Love You Better" and a vapid album entitled "Changes" before calling it quits. Both sank without a trace.

The Monkees were officially gone but they were not forgotten.

Chained together for three tumultuous years, the Monkees would soon be unleashed. Tork was the first to go. (Photo by Henry Diltz)

AFTERMATH

To say that the legacy of the Monkees loomed large over the respective careers of those involved is, of course, a gross understatement. In the following chapters, each of the four Monkees' individual stories will be chronicled from childhood to the present day. As a whole, the members suffered physical and spiritual hardships owing to the draining ordeal of their Monkees years. Although freedom afforded them time to recuperate from the stress overload, the word "Monkee" was destined to cast a long shadow over their subsequent lives. Being an ex-Monkee in the fast-food cultural wasteland of Hollywood was a prison they would find hard to escape.

In varying degrees the four ex-Monkees shared similar problems and predicaments. All four eventually saw their marriages end in divorce, had financial difficulties of some sort, and saw their careers stunted in some way by their Monkee past. At different intervals in time, all four attempted to disassociate themselves from their burdensome image as ex-Monkees, while ultimately coming to grips with the phenomenon that would shape their lives for years to come.

The closest thing yet to Monkeemania II (a.k.a., "The Bride Of Frankenstein"): Dolenz, Jones, Boyce & Hart.

Inevitably, the four Monkees lit out in different directions. Due to the abnormal pressures of their stardom, they had never really grown close as group. Now, after the split, relationships grew even more distant. Nesmith explains that, during the Monkee days, "when the press and the critical community put us in the category of bubblegum and meaningless nonsense, it was a hard thing for all of us to go through. We were constantly getting sniped at, which made it very tough in the inner circle. So whatever ordinary difficulties that would occur between professionals became magnified by the hostile environment."

Since the four personalities never did jell as a unit, a Monkees reunion has never seemed a likely occurrence. While many fans from the days of Monkeemania may wistfully long for such an event, there seems little reason or chance of it happening. When asked about such a possibility, each of the Monkees reacts quite similarly to the sentiments of Dolenz: "my answer is always 'if you pay me enough money.' I have no objection but I'm not going to do it for nothing. I always ask for a tremendous amount of money and they usually go away."

Dolenz adds, "the chances of it happening are very remote. The last time it came up Peter, Davy and I agreed to do something but Mike said no. I can't see Mike really ever agreeing to get back together." Indeed, Nesmith has become the "John Lennon" of the Monkees, thwarting every effort to reunite the original members. In 1975, when the four ex's got back together to consider offers from McDonalds and the "Midnight Special" television show to reunite the group, Nesmith

Boyce and Hart, who both auditioned for the Monkees, finally hit the bigtime with the 1968 smash "I Wonder What She's Doing Tonight". (From the collection of Jodi Hammrich)

Reunion minus one at the Starwood in 1977. Dolenz, Jones and Tork pose with Rodney Bingenheimer (with Monkees button) and various members of the Elton John band. (From the collection of Rodney Bingenheimer)

balked, demanding they do a movie instead. A possible tour was also rejected by Nesmith, who refused to play the old Monkees hits if such circumstances ever did eventuate.

Five years later, however, Nesmith did agree to appear with the others to present an award at the 1980 Emmy telecast ("It sounded like a fun idea," — Nesmith). Unfortunately, the award ceremony was cancelled due to an actor's guild strike at the time. Since then no other realistic offers have come to pass. The only tangible possibility for a reunion in the Eighties would seem to be on Nesmith's "Television Parts," although this, too, is highly improbable. Considering the fate of other well intentioned reunions — Crosby, Stills and Nash, the Animals, the Hollies, Simon and Garfunkel to name but a few — perhaps it is better that the Monkees left well enough alone.

Although the foursome have never officially reunited, the Monkees are hardly cantankerous enemies who spit at the very mention of each others names. In fact, the separate Monkees' paths have crossed many times since disbanding in 1969. In the early Seventies, Tork co-arranged a Dolenz single, "Easy On You"/"Oh Someone." Both Dolenz and Jones have collaborated on many projects, including a 1972 Bell Records single, "Do It In The Name Of Love"/"Lady Jane." The threesome of Dolenz, Jones and Tork reunited on several occasions, including their 1976 Christmas single, "Christmas is My Time of Year"/"White Christmas." The trio also united on stage — once in Disneyland in 1976, and another time at the Hollywood Starwood club in 1977.

The legendary Mayor of Sunset Strip, Rodney Bingenheimer, takes a spin in the Monkeemobile, the rarest of Monkee collectibles. (From the collection of Rodney Bingenheimer)

Over the years, a revisionist attitude towards the Monkees phenomenon has gained momentum. People who had grown up with the group paid no heed to the hoary charges of yesteryear — their memories of the Monkees were nothing but fond. In fact, in certain quarters, those, say, who deem the Banana Splits (a distant relative of the Monkees) the greatest rock band of all time (no less an authority than Joey Ramone has cast his vote for the Splits), the Monkees are utmostly revered. Still today, dozens of fan clubs throughout the world keep the Monkees' torch ablaze.

Japan has already witnessed the first full-scale Monkeemania II, which saw all of the original Monkee platters re-enter the charts. The entire revival in Japan was precipitated almost accidentally when "Daydream Believer" was used in a television commercial. The song became a smash hit all over again, and eventually every Monkee except Nesmith separately toured Japan. In the early Eighties, England and Australia have also experienced mini-Monkee revivals of their own, although nowhere near the mania generated by the hysteria-prone Japanese.

Surprisingly, even the Monkees music, which was so severely maligned during the Sixties, has undergone a revisionist turn-of-mind, with several album compilations, bootlegs and re-releases spreading the word. Critics, who savaged the group during the phenomenon, have finally realized the Monkees were responsible for quite a few classic pop tracks. Even the self-imposed authorities of the *Rolling Stone Record Guide* wrote that Monkees music "ranks with the best pop-rock of the mid-Sixties, which is saying something." Many new-wave bands have also bowed deferentially to the Monkees including the Go-Go's, Duran Duran, and Squeeze. Noted playwright Tom Stoppard paid homage to the band by including "I'm A Believer" in his Tony-award winning play "The Real Thing." The supreme irony of all this belated acclaim is that the Monkees are becoming more respectable than they ever were when they were together as a group.

Many of the other Monkees principals have fared well since their involvement. The notorious Donnie Kirshner carved an ignominious niche in American culture with the cartoon group the Archies. The Monkees debacle and the ensuing lawsuits, "absolutely blew Kirshner out of the water," claims Tork. "Kirshner thereupon left the Monkees and took up a project that was somewhat less threatening, the Monkees not being plastic enough for Don Kirshner — he went straight to the Archies, who were not going to give him any s-dash-dash-dash."

Under Kirshner's thumb, "Sugar Sugar" — a Jeff Barry tune previously rejected by the Monkees — became one of the biggest international bubblegum hits of all time. Later, Kirshner managed the rock group Kansas and hosted the popular late-night television show "Don Kirshner's Rock Concert" (which was properly hung out to dry by the wits at "Saturday Night Live"). Last reported word on the "Golden Ear" was that he was overseeing the film production of "Electric God," the story of Jimi Hendrix.

The masterminds behind Monkeemania, Bert Schneider and Bob Rafelson, went on to form the prestigous and progressive BBS Productions with Steven Blauner. Their first effort, "Easy Rider," was the counter-culture vehicle that catapulted Jack Nicholson to fame. In the following years, both Rafelson and Schneider continued to make their mark within the movie industry for their quality productions, including the award-winning "The Last Picture Show." Another BBS production, "Five Easy Pieces," won considerable critical acclaim for Rafelson, who both co-wrote and directed the film. Although he did not win an Oscar for this powerful treatise on alienation, Rafelson's "Five Easy Pieces" stands thus far as the highlight of his directorial career.

Schneider, on the other hand, did manage to snare an Academy Award, along with Peter Davis, for co-producing the Vietnam documentary "Hearts and Minds." The film, which faced enormous censorship difficulties in the U.S., was further embroiled in controversy by Schneider's hackle-raising acceptance speech at the Oscars. According to the *New York Times*, Schneider "inflamed the conservative wing of the movie colony. . . when he read a message from Provisional Revolutionary Government of Vietnam." In recent years, Schneider has kept a low profile, although he remains politically active, particularly in El Salvador. In the mid-Seventies, both he and Rafelson dissolved BBS; they remain, however, close personal friends to this day. In recent years, Rafelson has carried on his directorial pursuits while dabbling in the area of rock videos, such as Lionel Richie's "All Night Long" (produced, incidentally, by Michael Nesmith).

James Frawley, who directed the lion's share of the Monkees shows, and copped an Emmy in the process, has since maintained a successful directing career, including such features as "The Muppet Movie" and "The Big Bus." Although generally not given much credit for the popularity of the group outside the Monkees, Frawley is well respected by the members themselves. "When it came down to doing the show it was Jim," testifies Nesmith. "He was a real important creative force."

Chip Douglas (a.k.a. Chip Hatelid) has continued to write and produce records, including the reunion Christmas single by Dolenz, Jones and Tork. Douglas, whose production talents resulted in the most accomplished Monkees vinyl, was initially approached by Screen Gems to co-produce the Partridge Family with Shorty Rogers, but turned the offer down. Linda Ronstadt is among the artists for whom he has since worked.

The songwriting team of Tommy Boyce and Bobby Hart, responsible for many of the Monkees signature tunes, is no longer together. For a brief while, the duo managed to wrangle some teen adulation for themselves, via the 1968 top-ten smash "I Wonder What She's Doing Tonight." Despite the hit, they laboured in relative obscurity in the post-Monkees years until 1975, when they reunited with Dolenz and Jones to record an album for Capitol under the name of Dolenz, Jones, Boyce and Hart. Together, the quartet — which approximates the closest thing yet to a full Monkees reunion — toured American amusement parks with a show entitled "The Great Golden Hits Of The Monkees Show — The Guys Who Wrote 'Em And The Guys Who Sang 'Em." Later the group successfully toured Japan, where they released a half-hour video (produced by Dolenz) of their live act.

Dolenz, Jones, Boyce and Hart parted ways in 1976. Since then Boyce has relocated to England (as have Jones and Dolenz), where he still writes and performs. Hart, meanwhile, has continued his production career with acts like his wife Mary Ann Hart and the group, New Edition. "Over You," a co-written Hart composition featured in the 1983 movie "Tender Mercies," was nominated for an Academy Award.

DAVID JONES

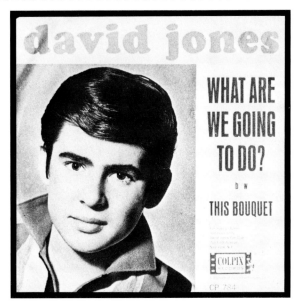

david jones

WHAT ARE WE GOING TO DO?

b w

THIS BOUQUET

COLPIX

CP 784

A pre-Monkees single from the guy with the dreamy smile and groovy bod. He even had his own fan club.
(Photo reproduction by Linda S. Johnson)

Of all the Monkees none was more popular than Davy Jones. Although his loyal following has often interfered with his private life — as in the case of his surreptitous marriage to Linda Haines — Jones has always been receptive to his legion of fans. "I'm not stuck with it," Jones says of his Monkees fame. "I feel it's up to me to be responsible to the people that inquire. When these little kids ask me, 'You weren't in the Monkees were you?' you can't say, 'Piss off, I don't want to talk about the Monkees.' "

Of course, at the height of 5'3", Jones could hardly afford to look down upon his many fans. A multi-talented man of stage and screen, Jones has always managed to utilize his pint-size frame to his advantage. "Quite honestly," he says, "from being a little kid in school I always felt special. I was always in the school play. I was always in the limelight, singing and dancing. My wife says that when I open the refrigerator door, I do ten minutes because the light goes on."

It was on December 30, 1945 that David Jones was born to Doris and Harry Jones in Manchester, England. Jones' father, a railway fitter, saw great potential in his son's abilities, although not necessarily in showbiz. Instead, he pictured his diminutive son as a big-time jockey. "When I was little, my father used to take me to the races with him. I always wanted to be in show business, but I was too shy to do anything about it, and I was too short as well, so I agreed to be a jockey," Jones recalled to *Seventeen*. "I quit school at fourteen and a half and went to work at a stable; I was always singing around the horses, which would drive the trainer out of his mind."

As an apprentice jockey at Newmarket Racetrack, Jones managed to ride quite a few winners but, alas, horseracing was not in the stars. "After a couple of years," Jones remembers, "the trainer took me aside one day and said that I'd never make it as a jockey — I was only five foot three but I was too heavy — and that if I went to London and tried to make a go of show business, he'd stake me."

Jones' knack for the stage had been exhibited at a very early age, when he made his theatrical debut holding the spear in the Christmas school play. His first professional job was playing a juvenile delinquent on a radio drama. From there he moved on to television soap operas and then to the stage. Only a teenager, Jones' star was on the rise — his cherubic good looks and natural stage presence made him a hot prospect on the London scene. His first big break came when the stage production of "Oliver!" — in which he portrayed the Artful Dodger — went overseas for a Broadway run.

Dickens, as it turns out, was Jones' lucky author, as he not only won a Tony nomination for "Oliver!" but won further accolades as Sam Weller in "Pickwick." The tour of "Pickwick" took him across the States, where he settled in Los Angeles to have a go at the big enchilada called Hollywood. Jones made a quick splash by appearing as a glue-sniffing wife-beater on "Ben Casey."

Eventually, he signed on with Columbia Pictures, which groomed him for future star vehicles. In the interim, Jones recorded an album's worth of material and three singles for the Colpix label, records he later described as "garbage." Nonetheless, Jones had, by now, garnered a respectable following, and his own fan club to boot.

Then came the Monkees. With his Columbia contract in hand Jones was practically a shoo-in. He has since revealed, in fact, that he was selected long before the other Monkees ever auditioned. "Not many people know this," Jones told *Blitz* magazine, "but that show was put together and written for me. I was under contract to Columbia months before the Monkees happened. I was at Mike and Peter's audition. Before I went into screen testing and rehearsing, my name was already part of the show, unknown to the other boys and sort of unknown to me because Ward Sylvester — who had been my manager since and signed me to Colpix — ceased being my manager at that point and became associate producer of the Monkees. I never told this to anybody before. I just feel it's right now because it's so far behind me that it doesn't matter."

Despite his shoo-in status, there was no guarantee that the Monkees pilot would make the grade. In fact, it almost didn't. "I decided that if the pilot didn't work out," Jones told *Melody Maker*, "I'd pick up my fork again and go back to shovelling horse manure in England." Luckily for both him and the Monkees, Jones was at the right place at the right time. A British accent in 1966 was worth its weight in gold. Almost overnight, Jones became the new sex symbol of the teen set, who fell head over heels for his dreamy smile and groovy bod. Having the lion's share of the romantic lead roles on the TV show did not hurt, either.

Jones displays his vaudevillian roots. "When I open the refrigerator door, I do ten minutes because the light goes on."

*Jones with Henry Gibson on "Laugh In," the adulterated version of
"The Monkees". Inevitably, his TV fame began to wane.*

The virtual mother lode of teen adulation did not rattle the twenty-year-old Jones, who said later, "There was so much of it, so fast, that to me it was no different than the school play. I didn't get bigheaded. I didn't say, 'I'm bigger than life.' "

Unlike Nesmith and Tork, Jones had no reason to rock the Monkees boat. With his smiling mug on every fanzine in the country, Jones was quite content to ride out his incredible wave of popularity without worrying about artistic control. "I was an actor playing the part of a rock 'n' roller," he later explained. "With all the pains that Nesmith and Tork were going through about being involved with writing more songs, I didn't really want to get my two pennies in then. I'm more a live entertainer. I like to be out in front of the audience to perform. When I do a TV show I like to be told what to do and when to move. I'm best directed — I'd rather not make the decisions, I'd rather be a part of the show." Jones quite openly admits he left his heart in vaudeville, not in rock 'n' roll. Perhaps the best example of Jones' vaudevillian roots is the wonderful "Daddy's Song" routine from "Head," in which Jones merrily hoofs in the great tradition of Tin Pan Alley.

Despite his popularity during the peak of Monkeemania, Jones never did much star-tripping in the swinging mod scenes of Carnaby Street or the Sunset Strip. "I like to be alone," he admitted to *Melody Maker.* "I play snooker or watch television or do some gardening. I don't like going to clubs. I think if we'd had to do the club scene playing guitars I couldn't have made it."

When it came to the radical chic of the late Sixties, Jones was pretty much a fish out of water. His roots were back in the quaint countryside of his native England, not a protest rally against the Vietnam war. "It's a funny thing," he told an interviewer in 1967, "I'm in Hollywood now, and I just bought a house for a hundred and fifty thousand dollars, but I don't feel as if I belong here. I feel that I belong back home in England. That's where I should be."

Jones did take one futile crack at in-crowd recognition when he opened trendy boutiques in

69

New York (Zilch) and Los Angeles (The Street). These were short-lived ventures and for the most part financially unprofitable. If there has been any one consistent aspect to Jones' career, it has been how he has handled, or mishandled, his money. Coming from a working class background, Jones was hardly a big-time wheeler and dealer. "We had limousines, Lear Jets, anything we wanted," Jones recalls of his Monkees days. "But I didn't go crazy. I didn't buy big Rolls Royces and silly houses. All my managers did actually — they all copped my money, but that's beside the point."

During the Monkees, Jones admitted, "money is important to me. When I was a kid in Manchester, we had an outhouse in the backyard and you had to take a bath in the kitchen. I don't have very much in the way of brains; I never had enough schooling. And my manners aren't much. Everything I've learned was from making my way on my own."

Unfortunately, Jones never developed much horse sense when it came to business matters. He revealed to *Blitz* magazine that "up until a year into the Monkees project I had no contract with the Monkees. The only reason I signed one then was because I was coming home to England just after the pilot for the show was finally sold. They wanted us to sign contracts, and I wanted to come back to England with some money, which I did. I bought my sisters each a car and a house in Manchester for my father. I needed some money and they gave me $15,000 and put a bunch of papers in front of me in my dressing room and I signed every one of them. 'Just sign it, Davy,' Bert Schneider said, so I did. Unknown to me at the time that meant $450 a week including publishing and everything."

Jones maintains an "anything is possible" attitude toward life. Pictured here with his family (l-r) Sarah, wife Anita, Jessica and Talia. (Photo by Susan Holderfield)

By the end of the Monkees phenomenon, Jones found himself holding the bag while the producers and sponsors made out like one-arm bandits. Despite a strong sense of pride, Jones is no longer resentful about the financial disparities of his Monkees days. "As far as the Screen Actors Guild and equity contracts and the rest of it, you really don't make any money once you've done it," Jones explains. "You make something on the reruns and that's it — the studio and the stockholders make all the money. Which is not a bad thing, otherwise some obscure person from a Tarzan movie in 1914 would still want to be paid and we wouldn't be seeing those shows."

Financial mishaps notwithstanding, Jones managed to maintain a high profile right after the Monkees break-up. In 1971, Bell Records released "Rainy Jane," a Neil Sedaka track left over from the Monkee days, that slipped into the Top Thirty. Meanwhile, Jones kept up his television appearances, including "Laugh In," "The Brady Bunch," "Love American Style," and "The Wonderful World of Disney." In 1976, he recreated the role of the Artful Dodger in a Los Angeles and San Francisco version of "Oliver!"

Inevitably, Jones' popularity began to wane, although the Dolenz, Jones, Boyce and Hart project briefly rekindled the flame. Even as his name became an entry in the "where are they now?" files of popular culture, Jones retained his sense of dignity and class. Ultimately, he returned to his homeland in 1977 to star in Harry Nilsson's musical "The Point," which debuted at London's highly respected Mermaid Theatre. Jones had met up with Nilsson in Japan where both were singing back-up vocals in a Ringo Starr leisure suit commercial.

Japan soon became Jones' home away from home in the wake of the massive Monkees revival there in the early Eighties. Throughout 1981-82, Jones toured Japan extensively, returning almost a dozen times to sing the oldies for the dedicated believers of Monkeemania. In attendance were "all those 12, 13 and 14-year-old girls who were there sixteen years ago," Jones says, "And they're still screaming, 'Daby, Daby, Daby!' " Still active, almost twenty years later, are the Davy Jones fan clubs, which shower affection upon their erstwhile teen-idol. "I get letters everyday through my door," claims Jones. "A lot of them say Davy Jones, England. And the postman delivers them."

Overall, Jones maintains the "anything is possible" attitude on life that marks his optimistic personality. These days, Jones resides on a farm in the Hampshire countryside where he breeds horses and trains for a possible Grand National competition. Currently he is writing an autobiography entitled *They Made A Monkee Out Of Me,* which will trace his life from his Manchester school days through the Monkees and into his solo career. "The names have been changed to protect the guilty," he jokes.

Unlike many jaded rock stars, Jones does not shirk his duties as an ex-Monkee, nor does he attempt to downplay his past. "I have a responsibility," he says. "I walk though the streets of London and I have a cabbie shout to me, " 'ello, Davy mate. Hey, hey we're the Monkees, right?' We're talking almost twenty years ago — hey, hey we're the Monkees? And people ask, 'doesn't it get on your nerves, isn't it hard to get away from?' I don't need to get away from it. It's something that's happened to me which every artist strives for — recognition — whether it be Rafelson's 'Five Easy Pieces' or Nesmith's 'Elephant Parts.' Whatever."

MICHAEL NESMITH

Michael Nesmith has established himself within the entertainment industry as something of an Eighties renaissance man. The list of credentials is certainly impressive — Grammy-award winning video director, host of his own network television series, producer of financially-successful and critically-hailed motion picures, recipient of gold records, winner of sports car races, multi-millionaire extraordinaire.

And a Monkee.

Not surprisingly, it is the latter credential — the Monkees — that surfaces most frequently in articles on Nesmith's accomplishments. Over the years, through countless interviews, the subject has been broached so many times that Nesmith has acquired something of a surly reputation for frequently debunking the Monkees in print. Apparently, his anti-Monkees image was merely a misunderstanding, however. "There is a common misperception out there that I have some sort of hostile feelings towards the Monkees," says Nesmith. "The only bad feelings I have about the Monkees are the stupid questions I get asked about it — questions of gross misinformation. But as far as the Monkees experience in my life, I had a good time. As far as the Monkees fans, I like them quite a bit."

From his earliest days as a Monkee, Nesmith exhibited a guarded attitude toward journalists. In his first Monkees interview, he told a reporter from the *New York Times*, "you're really asking me a bunch of rotten questions." To some degree that mistrust still persists today. According to Nesmith, "journalists want to talk to me about my past as a Monkee. Not interested. So they thing, 'well, it must have been a terrible experience.' But I'm also not going to talk about my family or about the cars I drive or my taste in clothes. There are certain things I'm not interested in talking about—the Monkees are one of them. So from that goes the notion that it was a terrible thing."

Due to his reticence in discussing personal affairs, the details of Nesmith's childhood are precious and few. What is known is that on December 30, 1942, Robert Michael Nesmith was born in Dallas, Texas to Warren and Bette Nesmith. "I had a wretched childhood," Nesmith once admitted to *Seventeen*. "We were dirt poor, just miserable. . . I hated school and I hated it at home." Eventually the family's fortunes brightened considerably when his mother Bette, a commercial artist, invented Liquid Paper (a.k.a. White Out, or typewriter correction fluid).

As a teenager, Nesmith led a troubled existence, a situation perhaps exacerbated by his parent's broken marriage. "I'm a streetfighter," Nesmith told Rhino Records. "Always have been. I grew up with hotrods and fists and all that horseshit." A sullen disposition at such a young age would no doubt have led to further complications had it not been for a simple twist of fate. After a firecracker accident in which an M-80 exploded in his hand, Nesmith began playing guitar in order to regain dexterity in his fingers. Music helped to forge a new identity for the Texas teenager, who could now channel his latent anger into artistic expression. In no time, the quick-witted Nesmith had honed his guitar playing skills and had begun to compose his own songs. One tune, "Go Somewhere And Cry," was recorded by San Antonio's Denny Ezba and the Goldens.

Music had become a full-time obsession by the time Nesmith entered San Antonio College, where his studied history. In short order, he crossed paths with two people that would significantly influence his life. One was his future wife, Phyllis Barbour, the other was John London (a.k.a. John Kuehne), a bass player. Together the duo of Nesmith and London began gigging around campus before branching out to a local dive named The Rebel. In 1963, after enjoying some local notoriety as the Trinity River Boys, Nesmith and London, with Barbour in tow, headed out to Los Angeles and the "happening scene."

The timing of this move was truly fortuitous. Nesmith's country and western flavored compositions were perfectly in tune with the burgeoning folk/rock movement in Los Angeles. Along with Bill Sleeper, Nesmith and London cut a folk single for the Omnibus label under the title of Mike, John and Bill. This line-up soon evolved into the Survivors, a short-lived band whse success was stymied when Nesmith's number came up at the local draft board. After a dreadful stint in Uncle Sam's Air Force (which saw Nesmith turn over a general's aircraft), he briefly joined The New Society, which featured future Monkees songwriter Bill Chadwick.

Eventually, Nesmith took a solo turn under the pseudonym of Michael Blessing, cutting two singles for Colpix Records (a label that, ironically, evolved into Colgems). Released in September, 1965, the first Colpix single, "The New Recruit," was a protest rant á la Dylan and Barry McGuire. A lukewarm review in *Variety* noted it was "still another message song with a routine melody and an anti-war lyric." The follow-up single, "Until It's Time For You To Go," by Buffy Sainte-Marie,

Michael Nesmith: Eighties renaissance man, multi-millionaire extraordinaire, and a Monkee. (Photo by Chester Simpson)

fared similarly to the first release — both singles never went beyond promotional pressings.

Despite the setbacks, Nesmith garnered a local following at such legendary watering holes as the Troubadour and Ledbetters, where the fieldings rock community gathered to showcase their wares. As as emcee of the Monday night hootenannies at the Troubadour, Nesmith rubbed elbows with many of rock's future notables such as Linda Ronstadt, Stephen Stills, Neil Young and later members of the Byrds, the Association, Buffalo Springfield and the Eagles. Many of those same musicians would also answer an advertisement seeking four "Ben Franks types" to star in a new network television series named "The Monkees." Although a dark horse candidate, Nesmith managed to lasso a role over his talented scene-maker friends. It was a stroke of luck he would later regret. "I felt like I got drafted," Nesmith told Rhino. "It was like being in the Army. I'd just gotten out of the Air Force — the most horrible experience in my life and I thought, 'boy, I'll never sign a contract like that again,' Ended up signing one."

Utilizing his crafty Texan instincts, Nesmith quickly staked out his own territory within the Monkees organizaton by demanding and winning the chance to record his own songs. In retrospect, however, Nesmith downplays his musical ambitions upon entering the Monkees. "I came into it from the standpoint that it was an opportunity to exercise some of my musical notions but, no, I didn't come into it as a musician," he says. "The idea that I was a musician caught up in the Monkees with a lot of talent but frustrated by three manufactured guys who had nothing to contribute is nonsense. Basically, I was about on par with everybody else. We were all trying to just muddle through.

"There are two common and, to me, repugnant notions about the Monkees. Number one, that I was the only one who had any talent, which is patently absurd. It's as unfair and as unkind as it is stupid. The other one is that I was the only musician. I wasn't the only musician and I wasn't much of a musician. Peter was a much more skillful player than I was by some orders of

Under the omnipresent wool hat, lurked an uncompromising sense of fair play. "He took his measure of it very seriously," says Rafelson.

magnitude. He wasn't a singer nor was he a writer. What I was able to do was write tunes — I could sort of pull those out of a hat. But they weren't very good, were they? I mean they were the tunes that were on the show from time to time, so that's what made them seem better than they were."

Nesmith's somewhat gruff demeanor and uncompromising sense of fair play became important confrontational tools during his many battles as a Monkee. One such example was the name he was originally assigned for the TV show. In the pilot episode, Nesmith was referred to as "Wool Hat," a name that would have stuck had the producers gotten their way. "He said, 'I will not be called Wool Hat,'" remembers Rafelson, who recalls Nesmith as being "the most independent" of the four Monkees. "He enjoyed the success of it, but he took his measure of it very seriously and said, 'I'd rather do it my way and have less.' "

Regarding his image as the volatile Monkee, Nesmith denies fostering an antagonistic attitude. "I don't think I was an angry young man. Specifically, not like James Dean or people in that poetic mode of rebellion," he contends. "I was self-conscious, nervous and ambitious. All those things transformed into a severity of countenance. But there wasn't any anger."

Nevertheless, Nesmith occasionally exhibited a hot-headed temper that resulted in several unsavory incidents, including the fist-through-the-wall confrontation with Kirshner. Other times,

"The only bad feelings I have about the Monkees are the stupid questions I get asked about it."

Nesmith was given over to deliberately provocative oratory such as his celebrated outburst to the *Saturday Evening Post.* His erratic disposition during the Monkee days might best be described as quicksilver.

An illustrative example of Nesmith's outspokenness is his quote from Jerry Hopkin's *The Rock Story:* "We wind up with the 11-year-olds who don't get along with Mommy and Daddy," Nesmith told Hopkins. "At first we rejected them, but then you come to see how they identify with the band. They're not articulate. We speak for them in a way beyond semantics. I mean, I love Jimi Hendrix's music. It's a very powerful statement of what Jimi is. Chicks hear Jimi and they've got to ball him. They hear us and what they hear in us is themselves. We're a reflection. There's no need to ball us when they can take the record home and it's like balling themselves every twenty minutes."

Even today, Nesmith rarely backs down from proffering his pointed opinions to the press. On the subject of the Monkees music, for example, he is not exactly indifferent. "I am not a fan of the Monkees music," he says "I have never have been a fan and I never will be. I recently bought 'More Greatest Hits Of The Monkees' that came out on Arista. I bought it, I played it, it's awful. It's poorly recorded, it's marginally played and they're weak tunes. . . I maintained from the beginning that the driver of the whole Monkees phenomenon was the television show, pure and simple. The

Monkees music on its own really had very little power and, in retrospect, that becomes clearer and clearer. All you have to do is sit down and listen to a Beatles record and a Monkees record — the Beatles record is breathtaking in its inspiration and the Monkees record is flat and uninteresting. But you combine that music with a visual image of some inspiration and they become supercharged. The minute the television show went off the air, the Monkees records meant nothing."

Nonetheless, Nesmith's regard for his Monkees days, in general, has taken on a softer edge as the years have passed. He now publicly acknowledges warm feelings and a certain guarded pride concerning his achievements as a Monkee. For many years, however, he was not quite as generous, particularly soon after the dissolution of the project. "It's like a blind man running for president," Nesmith said in regard to his solo career in the early Seventies. "I think you're gonna have to be a little bit better than the next guy to overcome that one handicap. I consider being a Monkee a serious handicap in terms of the serious music listeners. I consider it to be an asset in terms of merchandising value. So I greet the whole thing with mixed emotions."

"The idea that I was a musician... with a lot of talent but frustrated by three manufactured guys... is nonsense." (Photo by Henry Diltz)

Nesmith's assessment would soon turn out to be prophesy. Although his solo albums were met with critical raves, they made little impact with the record buying public. His first attempts were the most successful, a trilogy of albums with the First National Band. Enlisting the help of steel guitar legend Red Rhodes, Nesmith scored two Top Ten hits, "Joanne" and "Silver Moon." Next, he formed the Second National Band, a more eclectic group whose less accessible sound did not thrill Nesmith's corporate sponsors at RCA. In response, Nesmith went solo and recorded the sardonically entitled, "And The Hits Just Keep On Comin' ".

Despite a devoted following abroad, Nesmith laboured in relative obscurity in the States. Forsaking RCA and his L.A. base, Nesmith relocated in 1974 to the upper-crust arts community of Carmel, California where he founded the Pacific Arts Corporation. Along with his second wife Kathryn, Nesmith oversaw this multi-media company, dedicated to all forms of artistic expression. The first project of Pacific Arts was "The Prison," a progressive, almost overreaching, concept which combined the elements of recorded music with literature. Eventually it was performed as a ballet by a San Francisco dance ensemble. Financially, however, it was anything but an auspicious start.

Then, in late 1976, Nesmith stumbled, almost by accident, into the fast-growing technology of video. Island Records, his European distributors, needed a promotional clip for his new song "Rio". Nesmith spotted the opportunity to satisfy his curiosity about the uses of video. "I never had any notion of doing straight videotape," he later told *BAM* magazine. "Just standing up and lip synching to the song — that seemed idiotic to me. And I had no idea that that was what they wanted. We were talking about two different things. They wanted me to make a standard promotional film, and I had something else in mind."

That something else evolved into one of the earliest innovative video clips produced by a rock artist. With the help of filmmaker William Dear, Nesmith transformed "Rio" into a colorful extravaganza of surreal special effects elevated by a stylized sense of camp. Buoyed by the classy clip, "Rio" became Nesmith's first hit in over five years.

Realizing the import of this unexplored technology, Nesmith immediately launched head-first into video production for Kim Carnes and Juice Newton, among others. Such was his conviction that Pacific Arts soon discontinued "audio-only" records, concentrating solely on video projects. "You feel like you're in the presence of a power that's bigger than everything you've ever come in contact with," Nesmith asserted in regard to video's vast potential. "And I'm talking about a sociological phenomenon. I can tell you that there's plenty of evidence to show that the next Beatles are going to be on video record, plain and simple."

The providence of this lofty prediction, made in a 1981 interview, would soon be affirmed in the resultant video explosion in the entertainment industry. As it turns out, Nesmith had a hand in the creation of the wildly successful MTV format that revolutionized the business. Originally, Nesmith had produced a series of videos entitled "Popclips" for Warner Amex's initial foray into a cable music channel called Nickelodeon. Warner's later incarnation of this idea resulted in MTV, the trend-setting video pioneers of cable. "I can't say that MTV is an invention of Mike Nesmith's," contends Bert Schneider, "but it's damn near his invention."

Not to be outdone, Nesmith sunk his fortunes into producing a video record in 1981 entitled "Elephant Parts." Utilizing his past clips of "Rio" and "Cruisin'," Nesmith created a sparkling one-hour video variety show that combined both comedy skits and music to imaginative effect. For the first time since the Monkees, Nesmith also used his acting skills, creating a zany brand of comedy that subtly paid homage to his Monkees past. "I think if you're a Monkees fan and you look at 'Elephant Parts' you'll see a lot of throwbacks to what we were doing in the Sixties," comments Monkees director, Jim Frawley.

"Elephant Parts" did the trick for Nesmith, catapulting him back into the public eye. In 1982, he copped the first Grammy awarded for a video record and later was inducted in the Hall of Fame by the American Video Awards. Following these publicized successes, Brendan Tartikoff of NBC bought the pilot of "Michael Nesmith In Television Parts," a half-hour spin-off of "Elephant Parts." By the time that "Television Parts" debuted on network television in the Spring of 1985, Nesmith's career had truly come full circle — he was back on NBC in a comedy show, playing and singing his songs. Except this time, he wasn't a Monkee.

Never one to sit idle, Nesmith has recently branched into film production as well. His first feature, "Timerider," fared poorly at the box office, but his second, "Repo Man," became one of the critical and cult favorites of 1984. Although he has ruled out recording anymore "audio-only" albums, Nesmith's compositions have cropped up in "Television Parts" and "Timerider."

After inheriting 25 million dollars from his mother's Liquid Paper fortune, Nesmith gained the artistic freedom he has long sought. No longer beleaguered by his Monkees past, Nesmith has established himself as a forward-thinking man of the future. The advent of computers and the resulting technological revolution is of keen interest to the progress-oriented entrepreneur. Clearly, he is a man who faces the computer age with little fear. "There are certain classically valid things that are going to be around for a long time," Nesmith argues. "There's no danger of supplanting here. I can see an orderly, evolutionary progress that is mutally harmonious. I don't see some big technological juggernaut coming through and running roughshod over the values and treasures of mankind. That's not happening. What is happening is that we're getting tools, which enhance our own powers. So the power of the individual is just becoming larger and more enhanced."

Stay tuned for details.

MICHAEL DOLENZ

Originally a guitarist, Dolenz was forced to take up the drums. "Well, it's not brain surgery, is it?" (Photo by Henry Diltz)

"He always seems like the clown, but underneath he is also a sincere guy always ready to help a friend. He's a bit of a put-on, but always mischievous, never malicious. During filming and recording sessions Micky can always be counted on to break the tension with a bit of clowning.

White is his favorite color and educational and documentary shows are his favorite entertainment.

He's just an all-around great guy who's easy to get to know and easy to like. Hate is not a part of Micky's world."

—*Flip's Groovy Guide To The Guys*

More than any other member, Micky Dolenz represented the essence of the Monkees image. From the lunatic fringe of their comedy to the distinctive lead vocals of their biggest hits, Dolenz personified the spirit of Monkeemania — frolicking fun and freedom. As a master mimic who could imitate every and anything on stage, screen, or record, Dolenz became the Monkees jack-of-all-charades. An example of his adaptability was exhibited when, with no prior experience, he became quickly proficient on the drums. Years later he quips, "well, it's not brain surgery, is it?"

Two actors, in particular, were among those who influenced Dolenz's marvelous mimicry. One was the great James Cagney, a favorite impersonation of Dolenz in his Monkees days. He once told *Melody Maker* that "acting, to me, means portraying myself. Like James Cagney — no matter what role he was playing, it was just Cagney playing a priest, a crook or a pilot." Dolenz, too, exhibited remarkable chameleon capabilities, one second he was Maxwell Smart, the next Al Capone. His other acting inspiration was, no doubt, his later father George Dolenz, a respected character actor in Hollywood for many years.

Dolenz's free-spirited charm and effervescence attracted many fans. "It was the greatest thing that ever happened to me," he says of the Monkees.

Born in Los Angeles on March 8, 1945 to George and Janelle Dolenz, George Michael Dolenz was a showbiz kid with tinsel in his blood. It was at the tender age of ten that little Micky became a professional actor. Dying his hair blonde, Dolenz landed the role of Corky on "Circus Boy," a popular mid-50s kiddie show. Using the stage name of Micky Braddock, Dolenz enjoyed an early taste of network fame during the three-year run of the series.

Later, in his teens, Dolenz made appearances on "Peyton Place" and "Mr. Novak" but, for all intents and purposes, his TV career was in eclipse. Instead, he turned his attention to architectural drafting, first at Valley College and then at L.A. Tech. All the while, Dolenz began frequenting a club on the Sunset Strip called the Red Velvet, where he occasionally sat in on vocals for a pop group prophetically titled the Missing Links.

With the rock 'n' roll scene in full swing, Dolenz used his limited guitar abilities to full advantage. Besides gigging with the Missing Links and studying architecture, Dolenz formed Micky And The One Nighters, a Top 40 dance band that quickly faded into obscurity. Other musical adventures included two rarely-heard Challenge label singles recorded by Dolenz and later issued in the wake of Monkeemania. These tracks include "Huff Puff" and "Don't Do It," both featuring the guitar licks of one Glen Campbell. Despite a flurry of musical enterprising, Dolenz remained true to his theatrical roots, claiming later that "music was always a sideline for me."

As destiny would have it, music would soon be a main line in Dolenz's career, as he landed the role of a drummer in a new television series named "The Monkees." An actor first and foremost,

Dolenz, like Monkee cohort Jones, remained unfazed by the critical attacks levied against the Monkees' music. "It never really bothered me because I was not a musician. I was an actor playing the part of a musician," says Dolenz, echoing almost word for word the sentiments of Jones. "We were a television show first and then became a rock group. I quite honestly had no idea of what the music business was all about. I had never heard of *Billboard* and *Cashbox* until I had two or three records on the charts."

Surprisingly, despite his lack of musical expertise, Dolenz went on to contribute some of the finest original compositions to the Monkees, including the British hit, "Randy Scouse Git." Another stand-out Dolenz performance was the funky group-written "Goin' Down," which showcased his soul man vocal chops á la Otis Redding. Occasionally, Dolenz's vocal renditions were overly derivative, as in his dead-ringer Grace Slick imitation on "Zor and Zam." Nonetheless, from "The Monkees Theme" to the "Porpoise Song," Dolenz provided the instantly identifiable sound of the Monkees.

Onstage at the Monkees' concert performances, Dolenz became the show stopper, utilizing his irrepressible energy to whip the screaming teens into further frenzy. His James Brown routine never failed to bring down the house on the early Monkees tours. Besides being an incurable ham, Dolenz was an inveterate prankster, best illustrated by his infamous dive into the Hollywood Bowl fountain.

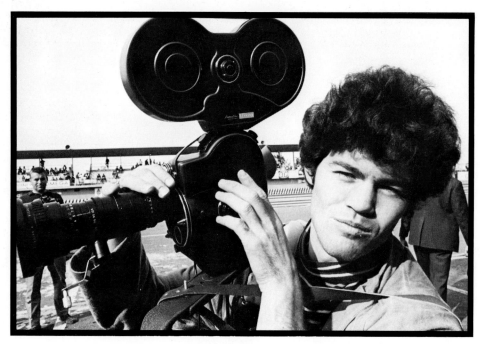

Born with tinsel in his blood, Dolenz was a network star at the age of ten. Directing was a logical extension of is talents. (Photo by Henry Diltz)

The true medium for Dolenz's all-around talents, however, was the TV screen. As the most gregarious and outgoing of all four Monkees, Dolenz was perfectly suited to the wild and wacky antics of "The Monkees" show. In the end, Dolenz found the TV show the most satisfying of the Monkees' multi-faceted ventures. "The thing I'm interested in most is communication," he told *Seventeen*. "If a parent can watch the Monkees with a kid and they can get to understand each other through sharing the experience, if we can bring them a fraction closer in any way, then I think we've done a great job and it will make me happy."

The inexhaustable Dolenz spent much of his free time as a Monkee constructing various bits of home-made whimsy. "I've always loved to do things with my hands," he told a reporter, "like working with wood. When I was a kid growing up in Los Angeles, before my father passed away about four years ago, he taught me to use tools. I've always loved that . . . Lately I've been fooling around with metal, soldering, brazing, welding. I just made my first piece of metal sculpture, and that means more to me than being one of the Monkees."

Occasionally Dolenz's handiwork got a little out of hand, as in the time he constructed a full-scale gyroplane, a vehicle similar to a helicopter. After painstakingly assembling the aircraft piece by piece in the middle of his living room, Dolenz realized it was too big to get out the door. As a consequence, the gyroplane became one of the few Dolenz projects never to get off the ground.

Since relocating in the U.K., Dolenz has gained a reputation for directing and producing. He recently filmed a segment for Nesmith's "Television Parts". (From the collection of Michael Dolenz).

By comparison, Dolenz was always the most accessible and approachable of the Monkees. Fans were attracted to his free-spirited charm and effervescent persona. His marriage to stunning British model Samantha Juste caused a great stir in the teen-zines, but unlike Jones' secretive union, Dolenz and Juste pulled off the affair with remarkable aplomb. Even after his career with the Monkees, Dolenz never failed to acknowledge his debt to the group. "It was the greatest thing that happened to me," he says. "There's no question of that. It did become difficult at one point to be taken seriously as an actor because everybody thought I was a drummer. But I have absolutely no regrets."

Indeed, Dolenz's career outside the Monkees was, at the outset, a decidedly up and down affair. The low point, like the other Monkees, followed the break-up of the act. "The industry is down on all of us because we didn't come through the correct channels and give everybody a cut in the action," he told Rhino Records in 1971. "It just happened overnight — BAM — from left field. So now we're paying our dues."

Finding his popularity at an all-time low, Dolenz took to working on animated cartoons, doing voice-overs for "Scooby Doo," "Devlin" and "The Funky Phantom," all Hanna-Barbera productions. Beyond a few cameo appearances on "My Three Sons" and "Adam 12," Dolenz's acting career took a swift nose dive. Among the roles he auditioned for and lost was Fonzie on "Happy Days." Other ventures included a B-grade snuff movie called "Night Of The Strangler" and a commercial production company that he headed. All the while, Dolenz attempted futilely to resuscitate his floundering recording career with a set of MGM singles in the early Seventies. Along with Mike Lloyd, Dolenz formed the group Starship, but unlike the Jefferson Airplane, the new name did not fly. Although a few of his subsequent singles, such as "Daybreak" (produced by Nilsson) and "Buddy Holly Tribute" were respectable efforts, Dolenz's marketability as a recording artist was six feet under.

In the mid-seventies, Dolenz hit rock bottom. His marriage with Juste was in a shambles while both he and Jones were locked in a bitter lawsuit with Screen Gems. Claiming they had never been fully compensated for the 5/merchandising royalties during the Monkees, Dolenz and Jones sued for twenty million dollars in damages. Up against the muscular corporate lawyers of Screen Gems, the pair ultimately had to settle out of court for a paltry $50,000. The strain of these ordeals had taken its toll on Dolenz, who later admitted he was "mainly recuperating" during these dog days of his post-Monkees career.

Dolenz's career did eventually begin to pick up steam. After the Dolenz, Jones, Boyce and Hart gig and a Vegas-oriented nightclub act with Jones (backed by the punk-rock band the Laughing Dogs), Dolenz finally returned to stage in Sacramento, California. The play was "Tom Sawyer" with Dolenz as Huckleberry Finn and Jones in the title role. Then in 1977, two events changed his fortunes. The first was his marriage to Trina Dow, the other was Harry Nilsson's musical "The

Point." Originally, Nilsson had envisioned only using Jones in the production, but at Jones' request Dolenz was written into the script.

"The Point" was to become Dolenz's last stage role, save for a brief sojourn to Japan during their early Eighties Monkees revival. "I just didn't have the desire," Dolenz says of his semi-retirement as an actor. "I had been doing it for so long, twenty years or more by the end of the Monkees, that I had no desire to be an actor or a singer anymore. That's when I began to think about directing and producing."

Instead of returning to his homeland, Dolenz decided to remain in England after "The Point" ended its run in London. There he was less burdened by his Monkees past than in the States. Enthusiastic audiences greeted his stage adaptation of the movie "Bugsy Malone" in London — a production he also directed. Dolenz also made in-roads in British television, directing the children's programs "Metal Micky" and "Luna."

Since relocating, Dolenz has managed to cultivate a growing reputation for producing as well as directing. Among his recent endeavors include a short film entitled "Balham: Gateway To The South," based on an old Peter Sellars record. Dolenz has also worked extensively with Britain's innovative Central Television, including a series called "From The Top." Another recent Dolenz effort was a comedy segment he directed for none other than Michael Nesmith and his series "Television Parts."

As for returning to his native Los Angeles, Dolenz seems doubtful: "Nothing about the business in the States really attracts me at this point. I think it's pretty mundane — especially television."

What attracts him to the British way of life? "A variety of things," he answers. "Initially, my wife was English and that certainly helped. My first wife was also English so I suppose I have always had an affinity with the British. Since then, I have become very fond of the country and the people and the heritage and the philosophies. They are also very receptive to my particular brand of humor and talent."

PETER TORK

Beneath the happy-go-lucky countenance of Peter Tork's screen character on "The Monkees," there lurked a subtle discontent. Unlike the other Monkees, Tork never embraced his celebrity status with any conviction. Instead, he took refuge in the narcissistic drug-wired lifestyle of the Sixties. The circumstances of Tork's man-made fame only served to alienate him from the outside world — a condition that would contribute to his latent alcholism. "Being an entertainer in my case was deeply involved with it," Tork says of his bout with the bottle. "One of the features of alcholism has to do with isolation. You feel you're not worthy of anybody's company. It's called 'arrogant doormat' syndrome and I had it."

Tork's immediate post-Monkees years were a morass of broken marriages, temporary jobs, substance abuse and law troubles. Thankfully, those years are now behind him, as is the bitterness he harboured over his Monkees experience. Like his cohorts, Tork has managed to put his Monkee past into proper perspective. "I had projected that I was going to be a musician in the group and when they started cranking out the records without me I was disappointed," he explains. "But I see now that it was critical — that's the way it had to be. A lot of things that bothered the bejesus out of me when I was in the band and after I left it don't trouble me in the slightest anymore."

Tork was a troubled youth with a remarkable acumen for music. "I was a punk," he says. (From the collection of Sandel DeMastus)

Born in Washington, D.C. on February 13, 1942 to John and Virginia Thorkelson, Peter Halsten Thorkelson was the oldest of the four Monkees. In his early years, Tork's family was constantly on the move, living, at different times, in Detroit, Michigan, Badger and Madison, Wisconsin and Berlin, Germany. Finally the Thorkelsons settled in Connecticut, where his father taught economics at the University of Connecticut. From the start, Tork was a bright but troubled youth. "When I was in junior high school, I was a punk," he once confessed in an interview. "I wanted people to love and admire me for my gentle wit, my talented music-making and my beauty of personality. Instead I was loathsome and irritating and quarrelsome, and I didn't know why people didn't like me."

Despite his troubles, Tork displayed a remarkable acumen for mastering musical instruments. At the age of nine, he started studying classical piano. Later he began fiddling with the banjo and acoustic guitar as well as becoming proficient at bass guitar and varied wind instruments. For three years, he honed his skills at Carleton College in Minnesota, but the constraints of academia were too much for the proto-flower power Tork, who turned on and tuned in before dropping out.

Eventually, he gravitated towards New York, where the Greenwich Village folk scene was in full bloom. There, Tork forged an identity amongst the hip and flip bohemians who flocked to Bleecker Street to emulate their poet/prophet Bob Dylan. Playing for pass-the-hat crowds in local cafes, Tork eked out a minimal existence while befriending such fledgling folkies as Stephen Stills and Mama Cass (although he was not a member of Mama's Mugwumps as is commonly reported). For a while, Tork did join the short-lived Phoenix Singers before tiring of the somewhat nihilistic and self-adulatory Village folk scene in 1965. In the interim, Tork had a brief, disastrous marriage to a woman named Jody — it lasted a mere three months before they called it quits.

Like so many soul-searching youths of the times, Tork hitch-hiked to the California coast with visions of splendor and adventure. What he ultimately found was a $50-a-week dishwashing job at the Golden Bear club in Huntington Beach. There he met up with his old pal Stills who offered Tork a role in his new band the Buffalo Fish. Tork accepted and for a brief while they made the rounds in L.A. Later, when Stills informed him of an unfilled position in a new television series called "The Monkees," Tork took a shot at the job and hit the bull's eye.

Fourth banana on the series and in the studio, Tork felt "humiliated, shunned and slighted. The worst thing was that nobody seemed to notice." (Photo by Henry Diltz)

From stories of his disheartening experience as a Monkee, one might conclude that Tork had no idea of what he had gotten himself into, but that apparently was not the case. "The goal was what you say," Tork explains in reference to the Monkees' overnight superstardom. "What happened was the goal. Nobody was taken by surprise. I wasn't taken by surprise by the magnitude."

"He had the folk frustration going," Chip Douglas says of Tork. Later, he would live out the quintessential hippie existence. (Photo by Henry Diltz)

It would not be long, however, before Tork began to feel the limitations of his creative license within the organization. While the other three Monkees performed roles that were marginally in line with their real personalities, Tork was forced to play a know-nothing numbskull. "It's a crummy game," he candidly admitted to the *Saturday Evening Post*. "But I signed a contract, so I'll play along. There are better games ahead."

Off-stage, the lack of musical control was insult added to injury. Although he was allowed to play fourth chair guitar on one of Nesmith's early cuts, Tork took the criticisms of phony pop phenomenon to heart. "He had the folk frustration going," remembers Chip Douglas. "He was the ethnic purist kind of guy who would rather have had more banjo parts and loved Pete Seeger."

Tork encapsulized his dilemma to *Blitz* magazine in a discussion of "33 1/3 Revolutions Per Monkee": "That show was innovation. When we were innovative, we went straight down the tubes. When we stayed with the formula, we went straight to the top. That'll teach us. Boy, I'll never innovate again!"

To compensate perhaps for his embarrassment and guilt over his involvement with the Monkees, Tork immersed himself in the political foment of the Sixties. "He was the first of the four to manifest any attitude about being against the war," recollects Schneider. "But he wasn't very far ahead of anybody." Of the four Monkees, Tork came closest to the image of a flower child, sporting the quintessential hippie style — love beads, paisley shirt, unkempt beard and a perpetually stoned smile.

Nesmith remembers a time when Tork's hip hippiness almost fueled a dangerous riot in Australia, where an anti-war protest had gathered outside the Monkees' hotel. "Peter went out on the ledge and flashed the peace sign," Nesmith recalls. "And the crowd started to go crazy because the 'V' for victory sign was a pro-war symbol in Australia. So here's Peter, standing there like some anti-war hero, flashing the sign the Yanks used in the Phillipines. I thought they were going to tear the place apart."

Along with political protest, Tork dabbled in the other staples of the late Sixties, including chemical enlightenment and a communal lifestyle. In 1968, he took out a loan and purchased comedian Wally Cox's huge mansion in Laurel Canyon, which quickly became a notorious refuge of ill-repute. The Tork castle was a rock star haven where every fantasy could be realized and often was — mass orgies were not uncommon.

"I have no idea how many rooms were in that place," reminisced musician Dave Van Ronk about Tork's infamous digs in *When The Music Mattered*. "But there must have been twenty, swimming pool, the whole thing. And it was wall-to-wall with crashed out hippies. In every room you had to step over zonked-out people, screwing couples, whatever... I was marvelling to myself at the enormous amount of bread that was obviously just going right down the tubes and at the enormous number of leeches and hangers-on that he had acquired and was more or less supporting with very good will. Nothing stingy about our boy Peter, by God. He was enjoying it."

"I was a very young man, and I lived through all that hoopla without a core. I thought it would last," Tork told the *Washington Post* many years later. "So I spent my money grandiosely, and other times I gave it away in abject humility. And what taxes didn't take went to unscrupulous persons of one stripe or another."

The last Monkee to be hired, Tork became the first to quit. After his contract obligations were met in late 1968, he announced his departure. The news was no surprise — Tork had wanted out of the Monkees from the very start. "I didn't want to hang out with those guys anymore," Tork explains. "I see now that I could have been perfectly content just being one of the musicians in the band."

The official excuse — that Tork was suffering from exhaustion — was no PR firm fabrication. "I think he just finally collapsed," Nesmith told Rhino in regard to Tork's departure. "A lot of people ask us, 'how did you get through the thing without going stark raving mad?' Well, the point is we didn't. Peter had it more pronounced... he was a very tired person."

Immediately upon leaving the Monkees, Tork formed the group Release with his girlfriend Reine Stewart. Release lasted for a year without releasing vinyl before disbanding. Tork later revealed that the group almost made the soundtrack of "Easy Rider" but was turned down. "We wrote a song for the 'Easy Rider' movie, a theme song, which unfortunately never came to pass," Tork told *Blitz*. "We played it for Bert Schneider, Dennis Hopper and Peter Fonda. They loved it but they went with McGuinn and Dylan. What fools they be! Ours was a much better song."

Without benefit of Monkee paychecks, Tork's bank balance began to tilt towards empty. In little over two indulgent years he had spent his Monkee millions. Now he was flat out busted. In order to retain his lease, Tork was forced to rent his house out to Stephen Stills who was in the formative stages of a new group with Graham Nash and David Crosby. In 1970, Tork finally sold his Laurel Canyon Shangri-La, whereupon he and the pregnant Stewart moved into the basement of Crosby's house. Soon after Stewart gave birth to a baby girl, the couple split up, leaving Tork on his own.

Things quickly went from bad to worse. Travelling through Oklahoma on a trip back to the West Coast, Tork was busted for hashish possession. The authorities, showing no deference to the former Monkee, threw the book at Tork, who subsequently spent three months in an Oklahoma penitentiary. Upon leaving the prison, Tork's record was wiped clean, but the strain of the ordeal had left many scars. Finding his former L.A. haunts hostile, Tork migrated north to Marin County, near San Francisco, where he took up odd jobs such as a singing waiter. There, he joined the Fairfax Street Choir, an aquarian age gospel choir that boasted 35 voices. Later he briefly bided time with another group named Osceola, after a famous Indian warrior.

After several years of aimless wandering, Tork relocated back to Southern California where he finally managed to assemble a stable home life. Now married to Barbara Iannoli, Tork had another child and landed a teaching job at Pacific Hills School in Santa Monica. For a year and a half, Tork taught social studies, math and music as well as doubling as a baseball coach. After his employment terminated, Tork tried another school but, once again, his personality clashed with the higher-ups.

In the face of dwindling opportunities, Tork decided to give showbiz another whirl. After making a few guest appearances with Dolenz and Jones, he lit out on his own. Various incarnations of repackaged Monkees oldies bands evolved, all with limited success. The most visible was Peter Tork And The New Monks, which briefly toured Japan in the early Eighties. Soon

Finally conquering booze, drugs and the "arrogant doormat" syndrome, Tork has pulled his life together. "I feel real blessed these days." (Photo by Michael Ventura)

after, Tork finally managed to put down the bottle.

"The bottom came for me in June, 1980," Tork recalls. "Then I managed to quit drinking. The following January I had my last toke of grass and last toot of snow. Since then my career has been puttering along at a steady rate." Once again, Tork relocated, this time to New York, where he formed the Peter Tork Project. His family stayed behind in Venice, California. These days, Tork can be found playing solo gigs at various clubs in the Northeast, where he maintains a small cult following.

Despite a rocky road since the Monkees, Tork remains fond of his past. "I learned a lot from and through the Monkees," he says. "I wouldn't have traded it for the world in terms of life and the experience. I feel real blessed these days. Partly because of the help I've received, I don't have to drink and drug anymore, which wasn't the case three years ago. I was in pretty desperate straits. I didn't know which way was up. I didn't believe I had a friend in the world. I didn't believe anybody loved me, except the kids, who had to. Now all of that has changed."

As for his three Monkee comrades, Tork harbours no animosity whatsoever. "I have an awful lot of respect for those guys," he says. "Each one of them in his own right is an enormous and amazing talent."

Back in the tumultuous year of 1967, Tork admitted to *Seventeen* that "no matter what happens — and I know it can't go on forever — I will always be one of the Monkees. Each of us will be that. Mike Nesmith, producer of records; Micky Dolenz, TV actor; Davy Jones on Broadway; Peter Tork, folk singer and soloist — we will share having been Monkees together for the rest of our lives."

MONKEES FILMOGRAPHY

THE MONKEES
Starring: Davy Jones
Peter Tork
Micky Dolenz
Mike Nesmith

Produced by: Bob Rafelson
Bert Schneider

First Season (1966/67):

1. **Royal Flush** (9-12-16)
Davy and the boys save the Princess of Harmonica from her evil Uncle Otto.
Written by: Peter Meyerson and Robert Schlitt
Directed by: James Frawley

2. **Monkee See, Monkee Die** (9-19-66)
The Monkees venture into a haunted mansion to claim their inheritance.
Written by: Treva Silverman
Directed by: James Frawley

3. **Monkee vs. Machine** (9-26-66)
The Monkees disguise themselves as kids to save a toymaker's job. Stan Freberg makes a rare appearance.
Written by: David Panich
Directed by: Bob Rafelson

4. **Your Friendly Neighborhood Kidnappers** (10-3-66)
Nick Trump, the manager of the rival Four Swines, tricks the Monkees with a series of publicity stunts.
Written by: Dave Evans
Directed by: James Frawley

5. **The Spy Who Came In From The Cool** (10-10-66)
Davy buys a pair of maracas with microfilm hidden in them, setting off a madcap espionage caper.
Written by: Gerald Gardner and Dee Caruso
Directed by: Bob Rafelson

6. **The Success Story** (10-17-66)
Mike, Peter and Micky help Davy look like a millionaire to impress his visiting grandfather.
Written by: Gerald Gardner, Dee Caruso and Bernie Orenstein
Directed by: James Frawley

7. **Monkees In A Ghost Town** (10-24-66)
Trapped in a ghost town, the Monkees are captured by gangsters. Lon Chaney, Jr. makes a guest appearance.
Written by: Robert Schlitt and Peter Meyerson
Directed by: James Frawley

8. **Gift Horse** (10-31-66)
The Monkees take up farming to save a little boy's horse. Nesmith's "All The King's Men" (never released) is featured.
Written by: Dave Evans
Directed by: Bob Rafelson

9. **The Chaperone** (11-7-66)
Micky dresses in drag to pose as a chaperone for Davy's date to the Monkees' party.
Written by: Gerald Gardner and Dee Caruso
Directed by: Bruce Kessler

10. **The Monkees** (Pilot) (11-14-66)
When Davy falls for the hostess of a sweet-sixteen party, madness ensues. Paul Mazursky makes a cameo appearance. Segments of Nesmith and Jones' screen tests fill out the episode.
Written by: Paul Mazursky and Larry Tucker
Directed by: Mike Elliot

11. **Monkees A La Carte** (11-21-66)
The boys, disguised as the Purple Flower Gang, thwart a gangster who has taken over Pop's Restaurant.
Written by: Gerald Gardner, Dee Caruso and Bernie Orenstein
Directed by: Jim Frawley

(Photo by Henry Diltz)

(Photo by Henry Diltz)

16. **Son Of Gypsy** (12-26-66)
Threatened with torture, the Monkees steal a priceless statue for a band of gypsies.
Written by: Gerald Gardner, Dee Caruso and Treva Silverman
Directed by: James Frawley

17. **Case Of The Missing Monkee** (1-9-67)
The boys foil the abduction of Peter and a nuclear scientist.
Written by: Gerald Gardner and Dee Caruso
Directed by: Bob Rafelson

18. **I Was A Teenage Monster** (1-16-67)
A mad scientist transfers the Monkees' musical prowess into the body of a monster.
Written by: Gerald Gardner, Dee Caruso and Dave Evans
Directed by: Sidney Miller

19. **Find The Monkees** (1-23-67)
A TV producer searches for the Monkees, who have tried unsuccessfully to audition for his show.
Written by: Gerald Gardner and Dee Caruso
Directed by: Richard Nunis

20. **Monkees In The Ring** (1-30-67)
A crooked boxing promoter tries to con Davy into a fixed fight until the Monkees swing into action.
Written by: Gerald Gardner and Dee Caruso
Directed by: James Frawley

21. **The Prince And The Pauper** (2-6-67)
Davy doubles for a prince to save his throne. Rodney Bingenheimer appears as Davy's double.
Written by: Peter Meyerson
Directed by: James Komack

22. **Monkees At The Circus** (2-13-67)
The Monkees walk the tightrope to save a small circus from folding.
Written by: David Panich
Directed by: Bruce Kessler

23. **Captain Crocodile** (2-20-67)
The host of a kiddie TV show sabotages the Monkees' appearance out of jealousy.
Written by: Gerald Gardner and Dee Caruso
Directed by: James Frawley

24. **Monkees A La Mode** (2-27-67)
The Monkees receive an award from Style Magazine but can't live up to their image of grace, chic and gentility.
Written by: Gerald Gardner and Dee Caruso
Directed by: Alex Singer

25. **Alias Micky Dolenz** (3-6-67)
Micky's resemblance to Baby Face Morales involves the Monkees with the mob.
Written by: Gerald Gardner and Dee Caruso
Directed by: Bruce Kessler

26. **Monkee Chow Mein** (3-13-67)
Peter opens the wrong fortune cookie and suddenly the Monkees must battle the evil Dragonman.
Written by: Gerald Gardner and Dee Caruso
Directed by: James Frawley

27. **Monkee Mother** (3-20-67)
Rose Marie makes an appearance as the Monkees' new tenant, who moves in when the boys can't make the rent.
Written by: Peter Meyerson and Bob Schlitt
Directed by: James Frawley

28. **Monkees On The Line** (3-27-67)
The Monkees cause a lot of hang-ups when they take over a telephone answering service.
Written by: Gerald Gardner, Dee Caruso and Coslough Johnson
Directed by: James Frawley

29. **Monkees Get Out More Dirt** (4-3-67)
The Monkees compete with each other to win the favor of April Conquest. Features the unreleased song "Steam Engine."
Written by: Gerald Gardner and Dee Caruso
Directed by: Gerald Shepard

30. **Monkees Manhattan Style** (4-10-67)
The Monkees save a Broadway producer from bankruptcy.
Written by: Gerald Gardner and Dee Caruso
Directed by: Russell Mayberry

31. **Monkees At The Movies** (4-17-67)
Bobby Sherman makes an appearance as a spoiled movie star who is replaced by Davy.
Written by: Gerald Gardner and Dee Caruso
Directed by: Russell Mayberry

32. **Monkees On Tour** (4-24-67)
A documentary look at the behind-the-scene madness of a Monkees concert in Phoenix. Includes some exciting but barely audible live footage.
Written by: Bob Rafelson
Directed by: Bob Rafelson

Second Season (1967-68):

33. **A Nice Place To Visit** (9-11-67)
Davy is captured by bandits after falling for El Diablo's girlfriend. Godfrey Cambridge makes a cameo appearance.
Written by: Treva Silverman
Directed by: James Frawley

34. **The Picture Frame** (9-18-67)
The Monkees unwittingly rob a bank thinking that they are making a movie.
Written by: Jack Winter
Directed by: James Frawley

35. **Everywhere A Sheik Sheik** (9-25-67)
To avoid a man she detests, a beautiful Princess tries to marry Davy.
Written by: Jack Winter
Directed by: Alex Singer

36. **Monkee Mayor** (10-2-67)
Mike runs for mayor to prevent corrupt politicians from turning the city into parking lots.
Written by: Jack Winter
Directed by: Alex Singer

37. **Art, For Monkees Sake** (10-9-67)
Liberace makes a cameo in this episode about art thieves who switch Peter's paintings for original masterpieces.
Written by: Coslough Johnson
Directed by: Alex Singer

(Photo by Henry Diltz)

38. **99 Pound Weakling** (10-16-67)
Micky flexes his muscles to win away Brenda from her boyfriend Bulk.
Written by: Gerald Gardner, Dee Caruso and Neil Burstyn
Directed by: Alex Singer

39. **Hillbilly Honeymoon** (10-23-67)
A girl's amorous intentions for Davy set off a hillbilly feud with the Monkees in the middle.
Written by: Peter Meyerson
Directed by: James Frawley

40. **Monkees Marooned** (10-30-67)
Peter swaps his guitar for Bluebeard's treasure map, setting off a wacky jungle adventure.
Written by: Stanley Ralph Ross
Directed by: James Frawley

41. **Card Carrying Red Shoes** (11-6-67)
A Russian ballet dancer falls for Peter, involving the Monkees in a spy ring.
Written by: Lee Sanford
Directed by: James Frawley

42. **Wild Monkees** (11-13-67)
The boys don leather jackets and motorcycles to compete with a tough gang of hoods.
Written by: Stanley Ralph Ross and Corey Upton
Directed by: Jon C. Andersen

43. **A Coffin Too Frequent** (11-20-67)
Ruth Buzzi appears in this episode about a seance in the Monkees' pad.
Written by: Stella Linden
Directed by: David Winters

44. **Hitting The High Seas** (11-27-67)
The Monkees sign on as seamen only to find out their captain plans to hijack the Queen Elizabeth.
Written by: Jack Winter
Directed by: James Frawley

BBC
V
Showing

45. **Monkees In Texas** (12-4-67)
The boys fight off Black Bart from the ranch of Mike's Aunt Kate.
Written by: Jack Winter
Directed by: James Frawley

46. **Monkees On The Wheel** (12-11-67)
Rip Taylor appears as the Monkees fight the mob after breaking the bank in Las Vegas.
Written by: Coslough Johnson
Directed by: Jerry Sheppard

47. **Monkees Christmas Show** (12-25-67)
The boys try to cheer a cynical boy (Butch Patrick of Munsters fame) during Christmas. "Riu Chi," a traditional Latin Christmas carol, is performed.
Written by: Dave Evans and Neil Burstyn
Directed by: Jon Andersen

48. **Fairy Tale** (1-8-68)
The Monkees spoof fairy tales. Mike is a cobbler, Micky a blacksmith, Davy a tailor and Peter a bum.
Written by: Peter Meyerson
Directed by: James Frawley

49. **Monkees Watch Their Feet** (1-15-68)
Aliens from Planet Spritz make a clone of Micky for espionage purposes. Pat Paulsen appears.
Written by: Coslough Johnson
Directed by: Alex Singer

50. **The Monstrous Monkee Mash** (1-22-68)
Davy's amorous desires involve the boys with Dracula, Wolfman and Frankenstein.
Written by: Neil Burstyn and David Panich
Directed by: James Frawley

51. **The Monkees Paw** (1-29-68)
A good luck charm brings nothing but bad luck to the Monkees.
Written by: Coslough Johnson
Directed by: James Frawley

52. **The Devil And Peter Tork** (2-5-68)
Peter sells his soul to the devil for a harp, but Mike wins it back in court.
Written by: Robert Kaufman
Directed by: James Frawley

53. **Monkees Race Again** (2-12-68)
Davy races the Monkeemobile to help out a driver whose car was sabotaged by the Baron and his Clutzmobile.
Written by: Dave Evans, Elias Davis and David Pollock
Directed by: James Frawley

54. **Monkees in Paris** (2-19-68)
Frustrated by the same old scripts, the Monkees shine off to Paris, where they are chased by four crazed teenyboppers.
Written by: Bob Rafelson
Directed by: Bob Rafelson

55. **The Monkees Mind Their Manor** (2-26-68)
Davy inherits a castle in England but must win a duel before claiming it. Tork directs.
Written by: Coslough Johnson
Directed by: Peter H. Thorkelson

56. **Some Like It Lukewarm** (3-4-68)
To enter a band contest, Davy dresses in drag. Charlie Smalls performs with Davy in the final minutes.
Written by: Joel Kane and Stanley Z. Cherry
Directed by: James Frawley

57. **Monkees Blow Their Minds** (3-11-68)
The Monkees turn the tables on a hypnotist, who thinks they are under his spell. Frank Zappa and Burgess Meredith appear.
Written by: Peter Meyerson
Directed by: David Winters

58. **Mijacogeo** (3-25-68)
Final episode in which the boys encounter a pulsing eye that freezes people to their TV sets. Dolenz directs. Tim Buckley guest stars.
Written by: Jon Anderson and Micky Dolenz
Directed by: Micky Dolenz
Produced by: Ward Sylvester

(Photo by Henry Diltz)

Head (premiere: 11-6-68)
Running time: 86 minutes
Starring: The Monkees
       Annette Funicello
       Victor Mature
       Carol Doda
       Teri Garr
       Sonny Liston
       Timothy Carey
       Frank Zappa
Written by: Bob Rafelson and Jack Nicholson
Directed by: Bob Rafelson
Produced by: Bob Rafelson and Jack Nicholson
Executive Producer: Bert Schneider
Assistant Director: Jon Anderson
Choreographer: Toni Basil,
Music Coordinator: Igo Kantor
A Raybert Production presented by Columbia Pictures

33 1/3 Revolutions Per Monkee (4-14-69)
Featuring: The Monkees
　　　　　Julie Driscoll
　　　　　Brian Auger and The Trinity
　　　　　Fats Domino
　　　　　Jerry Lee Lewis
　　　　　Little Richard
　　　　　The Clara Ward Singers
　　　　　The Buddy Miles Express
　　　　　The Jaime Rogers Dancers
Written by: Jack Good and Art Fisher
Directed by: Art Fisher
Produced by: Jack Good
Conceived by: Jack Good
Executive Producer: Ward Sylvester
Assistant Producer: Gene Marcione
Choreographer: Jaime Rogers
Musical Supervision: The Monkees
A Screen Gems Presentation on NBC Television

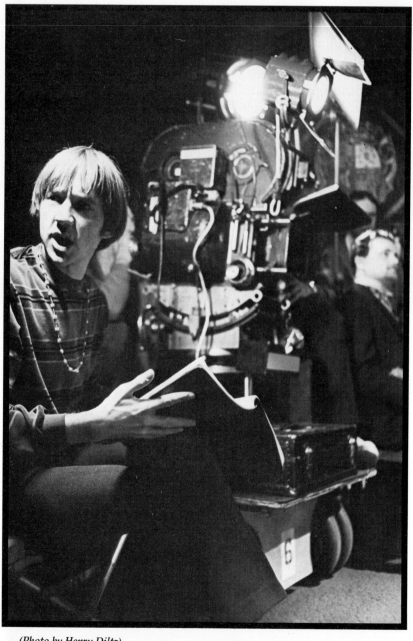

(Photo by Henry Diltz)

MONKEES DISCOGRAPHY

Monkees Albums:

"The Monkees" — Colgems COS-101
   Released: 10/66
   Produced by: Tommy Boyce
               Bobby Hart
               Jack Keller
               Michael Nesmith
   Highest Chart Position: #1
   Additional Info: Initial release album
   cover misspelling: "Papa Jean's Blues"

A

(Theme from) The Monkees (Boyce/Hart)
Saturday's Child (Gates)
I Wanna Be Free (Boyce/Hart)
Tomorrow's Gonna Be Another Day (Boyce/Venet)
Papa Gene's Blues (Nesmith)
Take A Giant Step (King/Goffin)

B

Last Train To Clarksville (Boyce/Hart)
This Just Doesn't Seem To Be My Day (Boyce/Hart)
Let's Dance On (Boyce/Hart)
I'll Be True To You (Goffin/Titleman)
Sweet Young Thing (Nesmith/King/Goffin)
Gonna Buy Me A Dog (Boyce/Hart)

(Album cover reproduction by Linda S. Johnson)

"More Of The Monkees" — Colgems COS-102
   Released: 1/67
   Produced by: Tommy Boyce
               Bobby Hart
               Neil Sedaka
               Carole Bayer
               Michael Nesmith
               Jeff Barry
               Jack Keller
               Gerry Goffin
               Carole King
   Highest Chart Position: #1
   Additional Info: Re-released as RCA RD-7868

A

She (Boyce/Hart)
When Love Comes Knockin' (Sedaka/Bayer)
Mary, Mary (Nesmith)
Hold On Girl (Keller/Raleigh/Carr)
Your Auntie Grizelda (Keller/Hilderbrand)
Steppin' Stone (Boyce/Hart)

B

Look Out (Here Comes Tomorrow) (Diamond)
The Kind of Girl I Could Love (Nesmith)
The Day We Fall In Love (Linzer/Randell)
Sometime In The Morning (King/Goffin)
Laugh (Medress/Margo/Seigal)
I'm A Believer (Diamond)

(Album cover reproduction by Linda S. Johnson)

"Headquarters" — Colgems COS-103
    Released: 6/67
    Produced by: Douglas Farthing Hatlelid
    Highest Chart Position: #1
    Additional Info: Initial release features different
    back cover photo with bearded Monkees

A
You Told Me (Nesmith)
I'll Spend My Life With You (Boyce/Hart)
Forget That Girl (Hatlelid)
Band 6 (Nesmith/Tork/Dolenz/Jones)
You Just May Be The One (Nesmith)
Shades Of Gray (Mann/Weil)
I Can't Get Her Off Of My Mind (Boyce/Hart)

B
For Pete's Sake (Tork/Richards)
Mr. Webster (Boyce/Hart)
Sunny Girlfriend (Nesmith)
Zilch (Jones/Nesmith/Tork/Dolenz)
No Time (Cicalo)
Early Morning Blues & Greens (Hildebrand/Keller)
Randy Scouse Git (Dolenz)

(Album cover reproduction by Linda S. Johnson)

"Pisces, Aquarius, Capricorn, & Jones, Ltd." — Colgems COS-104
    Released: 11/67
    Produced by: Chip Douglas
    Highest Chart Position: #1
    Additional Info: Re-released as RCA Victor RD-7912

A
Salesman (Smith)
She Hangs Out (Barry)
The Door Into Summer (Martin)
Love Is Only Sleeping (Mann/Weil)
Cuddly Toy (Nilsson)
Words (Boyce/Hart)

B
Hard To Believe (Jones/Capli/Brick/Rockett)
What Am I Doing Hangin' Round? (Murphy/Castleman)
Peter Percival Patterson's Pet Pig Porky (Tork)
Pleasant Valley Sunday (King/Goffin)
Daily Nightly (Nesmith)
Don't Call On Me (Nesmith/London)
Star Collector (King/Goffin)

(Album cover reproduction by Linda S. Johnson)

"The Birds, The Bees, & The Monkees" — Colgems COS-109
    Released: 5/68
    Produced by: The Monkees
                Chip Douglas
    Highest Chart Position: #3

A
Dream World (Jones/Pitts)
Auntie's Municipal Court (Nesmith)
We Were Made For Each Other (Fischoff/Bayer)
Tapioca Tundra (Nesmith)
Daydream Believer (Stewart)
Writing Wrongs (Nesmith)

B
I'll Be Back Upon My Feet (Linzer/Randell)
The Poster (Jones/Pitts)
P.O. Box 9847 (Boyce/Hart)
Magnolia Simms (Nesmith)
Valleri (Boyce/Hart)
Zor and Zam (B&J Chadwick)

(Album cover reproduction by Linda S. Johnson)

"Head" (Soundtrack) — Colgems COSO-5008
    Released: 12/68
    Produced by: The Monkees
    Highest Chart Position: #45
    Additional Info: Album coordinator
    was Jack Nicholson

A
Opening Ceremony
Porpoise Song (Goffin/King)
Ditty Diego — War Chant
Circle Sky (Nesmith)
Supplicio
Can You Dig It? (Tork)
Gravy

B
Superstitious
As We Go Along (King/Stern)
Dandruff?
Daddy's Song (Nilsson)
Poll Do I Have To Do This All Over Again? (Tork)
Swami — Plus Strings (Thorne)

(Album cover reproduction by Linda S. Johnson)

Without Peter Tork:

"Instant Replay" — Colgems COS-113
      Released: 2/69
      Produced by: Tommy Boyce
                 Bobby Hart
                 Michael Nesmith
                 Micky Dolenz
                 David Jones
                 Carole Bayer
                 Neil Sedaka
                 Bones Howe
      Highest Chart Position: #32

A
Through The Looking Glass (Boyce/Hart/Baldwin)
Don't Listen To Linda (Boyce/Hart)
I Won't Be The Same Without Her (Goffin/King)
Just A Game (Dolenz)
Me Without You (Boyce/Hart)
Don't Wait For Me (Nesmith)

B
You And I (Jones/Chadwick)
While I Cry (Nesmith)
Tear Drop City (Boyce/Hart)
The Girl I Left Behind Me (Bayer/Sedaka)
A Man Without A Dream (Goffin/King)
Shorty Blackwell (Dolenz)

(Album cover reproduction by Linda S. Johnson)

"The Monkees Present" — Colgems COS-117
      Released: 10/69
      Produced by: Micky Dolenz
                 Michael Nesmith
                 David Jones
                 Bill Chadwick
                 Tommy Boyce
                 Bobby Hart
      Highest Chart Postion: #100

A
Little Girl (Dolenz)
Good Clean Fun (Nesmith)
If I Knew (Jones/Chadwick)
Bye Bye Baby Bye Bye (Dolenz/Klein)
Never Tell A Woman Yes (Nesmith)
Looking For The Good Times (Boyce/Hart)

B
Ladies And Society (Boyce/Hart)
Listen To The Band (Nesmith)
French Song (Chadwick)
Mommy And Daddy (Dolenz)
Oklahoma Backroom Dancer (Murphy)
Pillow Time (Scott/Willis)

(Album cover reproduction by Linda S. Johnson)

Without Peter Tork and Michael Nesmith:

"Changes" — Colgems COS-119
    Released: 5/70
    Produced by: Jeff Barry
              Tommy Boyce
              Bobby Hart
              Micky Dolenz
    Highest Chart Position: Did not chart in Top 100

A
Oh My My (Barry/Kim)
Ticket On A Ferry Ride (Barry/Bloom)
You're So Good To Me (Barry/Bloom)
It's Got To Be Love (Goldberg)
Acapulco Sun (Soles/Albright)
99 Pounds (Barry)

B
Tell Me Love (Barry)
Do You Feel It Too? (Barry/Kim)
I Love You Better (Barry/Kim)
All Alone In The Dark (Soles/Albright)
Midnight Train (Dolenz)
I Never Thought It Peculiar (Boyce/Hart)

(Album cover reproduction by Linda S. Johnson)

Reissues:

"The Monkees Greatest Hits" — Colgems 115
"The Monkees Golden Hits" — RCA PRS-329
"Barrel Full Of Monkees — Colgems SCOS-1001
"Refocus" — Bell 6081
"The Monkees Greatest Hits" — Arista AL-4089
"More Greatest Hits" — Arista ABM-2007
"Monkeemania" (Australian Arista compilation)
"Monkee Business" — Rhino RNLP 701
"Monkee Flips" — Rhino RNLP 113

Repackages:

"The Birds, The Bees, & The Monkees" — Rhino RNLP 144
"Head" — Rhino RNLP 145
"The Monkees Present" — Rhino RNLP 147
(The rest of the Monkees' catalogue is due to be re-released by Rhino Records.]

Bootlegs:

"Monkeeshines"
"Polly Want A Banana?"
"The Monkees Collection"
"Rarities"
"Tails Of The Monkees" (note: be forewarned. Although billed as a live Monkees album, "Tail Of The Monkees" is, in actuality, a tape of a Dolenz, Jones, Boyce and Hart show.)

Monkees Singles:

Last Train To Clarksville/Take A Giant Step	Colgems 1001 (8/66)	#1
I'm A Believer/(I'm Not Your) Stepping Stone	Colgems 1002 (11/66)	#1
A Little Bit Me, A Little Bit You/She Hangs Out	Colgems 1003 (2/67)	(withdrawn)
A Little Bit Me, A Little Bit You/The Girl I Knew Somewhere	Colgems 1004 (3/67)	#2
Randy Scouse Git (Alternative Title)/Forget That Girl	RCA(UK) 1604 (6/67)	#2
Pleasant Valley Sunday/Words	Colgems 1007 (7/67)	#3
Daydream Believer/Goin' Down	Colgems 1012 (10/67)	#1
Valleri/Tapioca Tundra	Colgems 1019 (3/68)	#3
D.W. Washburn/It's Nice To Be With You	Colgems 1023 (6/68)	#19
Porpoise Song/As We Go Along	Colgems 1031 (10/68)	#62

(Without Peter Tork):

Tear Drop City/A Man Without A Dream	Colgems 5000 (2/69)	#56
Listen To The Band/Someday Man	Colgems 5004 (6/69)	#63
Good Clean Fun/Mommy and Daddy	Colgems 5005 (9/69)	#82

(Without Peter Tork and Michael Nesmith):

Oh My My/I Love You Better	Colgems 5011 (4/70)	#98